Be Seen, Be Heard, Be Memorable

Digital and Social Marketing Strategy

Customer engagement is the best way to ensure long-term success. The tools afforded by the digital age make it more possible than ever to enthrall your customers. Learn how to use the power of Content Marketing, SEO and SEM, and Social Media to create customers who are your biggest advocates.

by Amit Ahluwalia

~~~

Be Seen, Be Heard, Be Memorable: Digital and Social Marketing Strategy

Author: Amit Ahluwalia, Copyright © 2015 Amit Ahluwalia

ABOUT THE AUTHOR

Amit Ahluwalia is an author, entrepreneur and speaker whose career spans nearly three decades. Amit has a proven track record in leading corporate marketing teams, starting rapidly growing businesses and producing record sales. Leveraging extensive knowledge and experience, along with the ability to engage audiences, has made him a sought after speaker, author and business coach.

Along with numerous industry publications, Amit is the author of *Be Seen, Be Heard, Be Memorable: Digital and Social Marketing Strategy*, an insider's take on using social media, SEO, SEM and content marketing to engage your audience and grow your business. His second book, *Please Allow Me to Introduce Myself* will be published in late 2015.

He is the also the founder of Plans du Jour, a mobile app development company, and Brighter Pixel (BrighterPixel.com), a Social Media Marketing and Management agency. Today, Amit helps business owners, executives and celebrities capitalize on social media, SEO/SEM and content marketing using proven principals. Amit has been recognized as a master of campaigns focused on emotional engagement because…engagement causes action.

Table of Contents

WHAT ARE SOCIAL MEDIA, SEO, SEM AND CONTENT MARKETING?

To remain relevant in today's marketing landscape, you have to have a strong foundation in all forms of internet marketing. You need to understand how your decisions shape your current strategy, and be aware of what the future holds as well. Marketing in the twenty-first century is a moving target that consists of a balance between a relevant social media network, a strong content marketing platform, and an integrated SEO strategy to tie it all together.

Social media gets a lot of press in today's marketing world. Number of followers, likes, pins, tweets, all give a marketer standing in the ongoing competition to be seen, be heard, and be memorable.

- Are you using the right social media channels to reach your audience?

- Are your posts timely and engaging?

- Are people clicking through; in other words, are your social media tactics *converting* contacts into buyers?

These are all factors that need to be evaluated consistently and thoroughly. Your organization needs to have the elasticity to rapidly alter its strategy as the greater world of social media changes.

SEO and SEM are two acronyms that can mean headaches for marketing departments. SEO, or search engine optimization, uses the power of major search engines to elevate your product to the front of the pack. SEM, search engine marketing, is the financial investment you make in your optimized results. When managed and manipulated correctly, they can send a business soaring to the top of their industry. When ignored, they can leave them out of the all-important search engine picture. Any company that hopes to compete needs to rank high when a person does a search for their product or service. Especially when using search engines to market your product or service, you need to ensure that you're optimizing what your ideal buyer is looking for. It doesn't matter what it is, or how they phrase it.

Content marketing is that extra bonus that sets your organization apart from your competition. It is the mechanism that creates raving fans and passionate subscribers. It can be used as a lead magnet to entice potential leads to sign up for a newsletter, a conference, an online course. It can be a spiff to thank customers for their purchase, and make your company memorable. It can be a way to engage clients and customers in your mutual success. Or it can be a total waste of time. Choosing the right content for your potential customer base makes all the difference.

Throughout this book, we will be looking at examples from different businesses to show how large and small businesses can successfully employ a social media strategy. We will also be comparing product-related businesses to service companies to determine what strategies might work for different types of organizations. Ultimately, all companies require a different balance of social media, SEO, SEM, and content marketing to get their message to their customers, and most importantly to convert that signal into sales.

Like baking a cake, if you add too much of any ingredient or leave something out, your cake will not taste good. The same can be said for the correct balance of marketing tools. All of the elements have to be placed into the mix at the right time, in the right order, in the right quantity and consistency. How you do that will depend on your business and your understanding of each of your key ingredients. Let's start with some basic definitions before we delve into the details of each element.

SOCIAL MEDIA

Social is defined as seeking, enjoying, or taking pleasure in relationships with others. Media is defined as a means of communicating that reaches a broad audience. When you put them together, social media is enjoying a relationship with a broad audience. In the past, media was a one-way street. Since the middle of the fifteenth century, Guttenberg's printing press has made it possible to communicate with a large number of people. This could be done through tracts or bulletins, letters, newspapers, or books. But the reader was rarely in a position to communicate back to the writer. Therefore, there was very little social aspect to media.

In the twentieth century, both radio and television made it possible for people to communicate with a vast group of individuals using auditory and visual messages. But still, there was little chance for the listener or viewer to form a social relationship with the broadcaster. Communication, on the other hand, was limited to letters and phone calls. These were, for the most part, one-on-one devices, which were limited in the audience to two people, communicating with each other. In the twenty-first century, social media has changed all of that. Now it is possible for large numbers of people to communicate with each other.

It didn't take long for savvy marketers to exploit this new outlet, and use it to put their business ahead of their competitors. Now there are hundreds of different social media platforms, some with very broad reach, and others intended to communicate with a niche market. Knowing which social media platforms are right for your business is another spinning plate that marketing professionals must keep in the air. Keeping up with various forms of social media and ensuring that your presence is felt can be a major undertaking for any organization. To be successful with a social media campaign, you need to do the following:

- Identify Your Target Market

- Understand Where They Hang Out

- Establish SMART Goals

- Make it Easy to Link to Your Product/Service

- Make it Easy for People to Engage

- Analyze the Results and Make Alterations as Necessary

Identify Your Target Market

There's nothing new here. This has been the first step in marketing since cave men were trying to sell wooly mammoth hides. You should take the time to create a profile of several of your ideal customers. You should be able to clearly articulate:

Appearance

- Demographics: age, sex, gender, race, marital status, etc.

- Psychographics (What is their personality type, their stressors, their likes and dislikes?)

- Behavior (Are they social, private, gregarious, abusive?)

- Core Values

Location

• Where do they hang out (Could be in the real world, but mainly where do they spend time online?)

• What do they engage with (What type of media? Written, audio, visual?)

• What do they use search engines for?

Purchase

• How do they make buying decisions?

• What problems do they have?

• What solutions do they require?

Current Customers

• What do they like about your product/service?

• What keeps them buying from you?

• What sets your company apart from others?

• What would they change if they could?

Persona

• What is the name of your ideal customer (give him/her a name that your organization can identify with)?

• Come up with a visual representation of the typical customer, either a real photo or an illustration.

• Make sure everyone in the organization knows this "person" and can identify with them and identify them when they meet them.

Where Do They Hang Out?

Now that you have a buyer persona, it's a lot easier to determine where they spend time online. This is something that needs to be evaluated and revisited at least quarterly to make sure you're still relevant. Especially if you're marketing to people in the 18 to 24-year-old age group. Remember, people move in and out of this demographic all the time. The place today's twenty-four-year-olds hang out will not be the place tomorrow's eighteen-year-olds visit. If you have to, hire an intern that just graduated from high-school to keep you apprised of the latest social media hotspots and how to use them.

Even if your ideal buyer persona is forty-three-year-old, divorced, vegan, soccer-mom who lives in an intentional community, don't become complacent. Make sure you know where she is hanging out, and what is new in her world at all times.

<u>Establish SMART Goals</u>

- Specific

- Measurable

- Attainable

- Relevant

- Time Bound

Is your goal *Specific*?

- To gain 525 new followers per month on Twitter.

- To have 10% more followers on LinkedIn than competitor _____ by the third quarter.

- To get increase click through by 25% this month on new Facebook campaign.

If your goal looks like this, it is not specific

- To get a lot of followers on Twitter.

- To have a successful ad campaign on Facebook.

Is your goal *Measurable*?

- To gain **525 new** followers per month on Twitter.

- To have **10% more** followers on LinkedIn than competitor _____ by the third quarter.

- To get increase click through by **25%** this month on new Facebook campaign.

Is your goal *Attainable*?

- That all depends on your business.

- If you set your goals so high they can't be obtained, then you will demoralize your team.

- If they are too easy, they won't be a challenge, and there won't be any reward for achieving it.

Is your goal *Relevant*?

That depends on your organization and what you know about your customers. If your target customer has never heard of Twitter, and your goal is to gain 525 new followers per month, then your goal is probably not relevant. You're either wasting your time, or you don't really know your customers. Either way, something needs to change.

Is your goal *Time-Bound*?

- To gain 525 new followers **per month** on Twitter.

- To have 10% more followers on LinkedIn than competitor _____ **by the third quarter.**

- To get increase click through by 25% **this month** on new Facebook campaign.

Make it Easy to Link to Your Product or Service

Make sure your post on social media has a clear relationship to the landing page for your product or service. People are busy, they have a million distractions, and they don't have time to click from page to page. If you want your social media campaign to be a success, you need to get them to a relevant landing page where they can make a purchase with one click.

This is especially important for people who are doing mobile searches. Mobile searches are increasing at such an astounding rate, it's impossible to provide any relevant statistics that will remain evergreen. All you need to know is that people using mobile devices (smartphones and tablets) to surf the internet is huge. This is not going to change, in fact, it is likely to become more and more common. People from all demographics are now routinely using their mobile devices to perform searches wherever they are, whenever they are.

The biggest issue with mobile searches is speed. Often times they are slower to load than a pc or laptop. That means that if they have to go from page to page searching for a way to purchase, you are going to lose even more customers. Size is also a factor. You need to make sure that your landing page is optimized for mobile devices. This means that if a customer pulls up your site on a mobile device, they are able to see all of the relevant information. It has to look good even though the screen is much smaller, has a different aspect ratio, or is in portrait instead of landscape.

Make it Easy for People to Engage

The best way to gain traction for your social media campaign is to get your clients and customers to do the marketing for you. Get them engaged and invested in the success of your campaign. The best way to do this is to solve their problem in such an effective way that they become advocates for you. And to make them an integral part of the solution.

When people are genuinely enthralled with your content, they become passionate about your business and about the partnership. They want to more fully engross themselves in that experience. They wish to share that experience with others.

Think about a time when you learned something, saw something, felt something so powerful that you wanted to tell everyone you knew about it. You were proud and excited to spread the word because you knew other people would be as enthralled by it as you were. That's the kind of campaign you should strive to produce. This is called engagement, and engagement causes action.

Analyze the Results

Every campaign needs to be analyzed on a regular basis to make sure it is still relevant and still getting the results you anticipated. Fortunately, there are numerous social media analytics platforms available that can make this relatively straightforward.

No matter what social media outlet you're using to set up an advertising campaign, it's essential that you evaluate the performance while it's running and after it's finished. Make tweaks as necessary during the campaign to improve overall results. The flexibility and relatively low cost of entry for social media makes this not only possible but necessary.

SEO/SEM

The next part of a twenty-first century online marketing campaign should involve SEO and SEM management. SEO stands for search engine optimization, and SEM stands for search engine marketing. They go hand-in-hand to make sure customers who are using the internet to find the product or service you sell, find you.

There are three major search engines, Google, Bing, and Yahoo. They have become the go to for answers to every question you can think of. They combine the functionality of the phone book, a library, a dictionary, an encyclopedia, and any other reference people used to use. Now with a few keystrokes, or even a voice command, people can obtain answers to their questions.

If their question is, "where can I buy (your product/service)?" you want to make sure your name comes up at the top of the list. There are some ways to do this, which will be discussed more thoroughly in a future chapter. But just like with everything else in the online marketing world, SEO management has become a moving target. The rules are constantly changing to provide more and more relevant searches. Some rules that prevailed three years ago are not only obsolete, but they could also actually damage your efforts.

The reason for all this change is that the search engines are businesses, like any other. They are in the business of providing the best possible answer to people's questions. They are rewarded for providing good answers by having more and more people visit their site, and by having people pay to advertise on that site. Google is by far the best example of this, and they drive the search engine industry. What they want are happy Google customers. The way they get a happy customer is by providing relevant answers.

In the past, it was common for marketers to attempt to rise in the ranks of Google searches by "keyword stuffing"— placing particular words in their marketing materials that would rank them higher in the Google search, even though the actual content had nothing to do with that keyword. People would go to that page, and not find what they were looking for. This didn't make Google or their customers happy. So now Google punishes companies for "keyword stuffing."

It's important to understand all of the things that make you appear higher on a Google search in a legitimate manner and to avoid situations that might lead to a lower ranking by Google.

SEM or search engine marketing is using a search engine such as Google as your online marketing partner. Google sells spots one through three on their results pages for companies. However, you have to prove that your content meets certain criteria before they will allow you to buy this valuable ad space. If you're approved, your website or web page will come up as one of the top three options on Google, with a little yellow square that says ad. Then you will pay Google an agreed upon amount each time a customer clicks through to your page. This is called PPC or pay per click.

- Relevance

- Good Customer Experience

- Good Value

Google evaluates the site to make sure that your keywords are relevant based on what you are actually selling. For instance if someone searches for "women's blouses," it would not be pertinent to take them to a Mercedes-Benz dealership. Google is constantly evaluating the "click-through rate." If no one ever clicks on your ad, then they assume it must not be what people are looking for in their search, and you will get a lower ranking. They also look at the landing page. Is it easy to navigate? Is the content straightforward? They want someone who comes to Google to wind up with the best possible answer, each and every time.

They also look at ad formatting. Does the advertiser include critical information like address and phone number? Do they have a brief summary of the site, that lets people know what they are getting before they click through? All these things matter to Google and are included in your search engine ranking. If you do a superb job of optimizing your content and your ad, you can obtain a much higher ranking at a lower cost per click.

CONTENT MARKETING

The final piece of the online marketing puzzle is content marketing. This is not a new strategy that has just appeared with the dawn of social media, but it has been taken to a new level. Content marketing primarily consists of creating an ancillary product that is given away to a customer to help support the product that you want them to buy. One of the earliest examples was Jell-O gelatin, giving away cookbooks to customers detailing all of the deserts they could make. Of course, this was not only a benefit to the client, but it spurred sales of Jell-O by giving people ideas about how to use the product. The same is even truer today. And with the technology available, it's even easier to create outstanding content.

Some of the Benefits of Content Marketing:

• Great, relevant content increases your SEO ranking. It makes Google jubilant, and in turn you are rewarded for supplying it.

- It sells your product without selling by creating an obligatory sense of value in the customer's mind.

- It increases brand awareness while providing value.

- It can act as a lead magnet to increase your e-mail list.

- It generates customer loyalty and retention.

Some Examples of Content Marketing

- Blog with "How to" Posts.

- E-books

- Guides

- YouTube DIY Videos

- Podcasts

- Webinars

- Classes/Training

- Templates

- Infographics

- White Papers

- Coupons

All of these things not only help your SEO ranking in a purely organic and above board way, but they also make you look like a hero to the customer. This keeps them coming back for more and gets them engaged in selling your product for you.

Content marketing along with social media and SEO/SEM work together in the digital age to create a marketing strategy that gets you seen, gets you heard, and makes you memorable.

DEFINE YOUR GOALS AND STRATEGY FOR EACH CAMPAIGN

POTENTIAL GOALS FOR MARKETING CAMPAIGNS

In Chapter One, we discussed SMART Goals, why they are important, and how to set them. In this chapter, we are going to look at several different types of campaigns designed to accomplish various goals. We will also consider what role social media, SEO/SEM, and content marketing play in realizing those objectives.

- Generate Leads

- Demonstrate Products/Features

- Customer Support or Service

- Feedback on Potential Product Enhancements

- Recruit New Employees

- Change Perception of Your Brand/Image

- Increase Followers on a Social Platform

We will define each of the goals and provide an example of how to use a piece of specially developed content. It will be combined with a social media campaign, and SEO/SEM, to ensure your goal is not only realized, but your company is seen, heard, and memorable.

Generate Leads

Using an online marketing strategy is one of the best ways to generate leads for your product or service. A lead is simply a person who has been identified as someone who is willing to be marketed to. For some reason, the "lead" has shown an interest in your product, and they are ready to hear more about your product or service. Therefore, qualified leads are a very valuable thing for any organization to have.

In the past, people used to buy leads, which frequently consisted of a mailing list. The marketer would then mail out their materials to the people on the list as part of a direct marketing campaign. Most people refer to this as "junk mail" for a reason. Sometimes you get something you really want in your mailbox, but often times it goes straight to the trash.

Savvy marketers who use a combination of social media, SEO/SEM, and content marketing can generate more high-quality leads. They can establish an e-mail list of customers who are eager to hear from them, and who will undoubtedly be converted to clients when the time is right.

The first step is to create your content, which, in this case, is going to be called a "lead magnet." It's a piece of specially designed content which is provided for free in exchange for some information about the customer.

Demonstrate Products/Features

One of the best ways to show your product or features in the digital age is by using online marketing strategy. With services available such as YouTube, it has never been easier to provide your customers with an easy-to-follow demonstration. Providing buyers with easy-to-follow illustrations means they understand your product or service before they buy it. Demonstrations can allow them to utilize the product and become excited and invested in it, and in its success within their organization.

In the past, marketers had to depend on things like trade shows, door-to-door sales, or floor models to demonstrate their products. But now it's possible to do online demonstrations that can in turn generate leads and captivate attention.

Customer Support and Service

Online marketing can be used to provide customer support and service. Using a content piece like a customer consultation can increase customer engagement with a product and establish a strong relationship between your company and your customer.

But, by far the most exciting opportunity for customer support and customer service lies in the ability to perform transparent engagements across platforms like Twitter, Facebook, Google+, or even Instagram.

The fact is that customers are already using these platforms to make complaints, raise issues, and vent their frustrations. One of the biggest threats of the digital age is earning a bad reputation from customer complaints that are broadcast to all corners of the earth. But right now, relatively few organizations are addressing these issues online. They let the complaints slip through the cracks, or perhaps they don't notice them at all.

The customer in this situation undoubtedly feels abandoned and ignored. Also, everyone with access to their social network or the network of the company in question can now see their complaint and the lack of response from the company. This is an enormous opportunity for companies to step up and make things right in a very public forum.

Imagine the impact it would make on the Twitterverse if someone complained about bad service at a retail store, and immediately a representative came online to apologize. What if the customer and the agent talked through the situation, and came to a mutually satisfactory conclusion. All of this while people from the customer and the company's Twitter feeds were rolling along.

And then after the problem was solved, that whole transaction remained in the client and the firm's feed eternally. Anyone could pull it up anytime. That would be so much better than what typically happens now. Have you ever looked at a big company's Twitter feed or YouTube channel and seen all kinds of customer complaints, none of which were ever addressed? Does it make you feel like doing business with that company?

This is an excellent opportunity, not only to provide real-time customer service but to ensure that everyone in the social media world has a good impression of your company.

Feedback on Potential Product Enhancements

One of the best ways to secure those passionate customers is to make them involved in the process of your marketing and product development. Asking your customers for feedback is also the best way to fine tune your customer profiles. By staying current on who your customers are and what they are looking for you can ensure that your products continue to meet their needs.

And if you're developing new products without the benefit of customer feedback, then you are wasting time and money. The beauty of the internet and social media is that there are millions of people just begging to be asked what they want, how they feel, what they like, what they don't like. Creating a personal, targeted survey or request for feedback is a great way to determine what direction your company should head.

Recruit New Employees

Another way forward-thinking companies are using their internet marketing strategies is to recruit the best employees.

No longer is it necessary to hire headhunters who charge thousands of dollars to find the right applicants. These people are online like everyone else. If you have an online presence as a culture people want to work for, you will have all the top-notch applicants you could ever need.

Having a clean, progressive, fully responsive, and socially interactive careers page on your website is the best way to demonstrate that you are a forward-thinking company. You can also use platforms like LinkedIn as the ideal recruitment tool. This network is actually developed with the idea of job seeking in mind. It is ideally suited for both people looking for jobs, and companies looking for employees. If your campaign involves hiring, a LinkedIn advertisement should definitely be part of your strategy.

Change the Perception of your Brand or Image

You may need to change the perception or image of your brand. Perhaps there was a high-profile recall of one of your products. Or possibly, your image has just become rather tired and outdated. Using social media marketing is an excellent way to revitalize or reinvent your image.

A wonderful example of using social media to change brand image comes from the CEO of BlendTec, a company that specializes in blenders. He's the host of a popular video series in which he tests his blenders on everyday items to see if they will blend. His videos have well over 125 million views, which probably translated to more than a few blender sales while changing his company image.

Increase Your Followers

Without impactful, consistent content and adequate SEO/SEM management, a significant number of followers will not have a great deal of impact. However, if you incorporate a large number of followers into an overall strategy, it can indicate a high-level of authority that builds upon itself.

On the other hand, having great content and a robust SEO/SEM strategy won't get you very far if you don't have anyone enlisted in your network. The right combination of an engaged, active, and vocal community to take advantage of and help broadcast your content is a key to success.

CONTENT MARKETING TOOLS TO REACH YOUR GOALS

In this chapter, we will discuss a variety of content marketing tools to help you reach your campaign goals.

- Blog

- E-books

- Guides

- YouTube Videos

- Podcasts

- Webinars

- Classes

- Templates

- Infographics

- Slides

- White Papers

- Coupons

Providing the right content, at the right time, for the right type of campaign is the best way to magnetize followers. There are many types of content that can be used to meet the goals of your online campaign described above. Each of them has benefits, and drawbacks. Not all of them are right for any one type of campaign, or several of them may be used in combination.

Blog

The blog has been around for well over ten years. It has been used to provide meaningful content that has helped establish brand leadership, and has also proved embarrassing. If you decide to use a blog as part of your content marketing strategy, be aware that to be done right, it takes a lot of time, and top-notch writing skills. If your blog is inconsistent, or poorly written, it will do the opposite of what you hope for with content marketing, and actually harm your business.

Steps to blog proficiency

• Hire someone whose job or part of their job is to write and manage your blog content. If you can't afford someone full time, or even part time to do the writing, farm the articles out to your social media agency.

• Create an ongoing content calendar that has a running six months of articles planned out. This will allow you to see where your internal staff can provide the writing resources and where you need to outsource.

• Stick to your calendar, but build in enough flexibility to allow for last minute changes driven by market fluctuations. (Never just chuck the calendar!)

• Don't overextend yourself. If you can only commit to one post per week, then do one post per week, every week, 52 weeks per year.

• If you do less than one per week, the content needs to be stellar, and worth the wait. People have so many distractions that they lose reference to things they don't see at least weekly.

• It should go without saying, but make sure the content reflects your company values. That includes spelling and grammar errors.

• Give your readers a reason to comment and become part of the conversation. Write content that encourages discussion, opinions, even arguments. Ask your reader to share their experiences, values, and views.

E-Books

E-books are great content to offer as a lead magnet, or a boost to your content credentials. They are relatively inexpensive and have a great Wow! factor. If you don't have someone in your company with the skills and resources to write a book, your social media agency can provide a ghostwriter as part of your content marketing engagement.

Steps to E-book Proficiency

• Determine what content you need to fit your marketing strategy.

• Make sure your book is fairly evergreen. That way you will be able to use it for a long time and it will stay relevant.

• Make sure the writing is solid, and the tone reflects your organization. The tone of a book for a law firm will be a lot different from that of a coffee shop.

• Examples

— Real Estate Agent- How to Simplify Your Life before Your Move

— Investment Firm- How to Plan for Retirement

— Clothing Retailer- Essentials for Every Professional's Wardrobe

— Veterinarian- Common Health Issues by Dog Breed

Guides/Cheat Sheets

Some of the easiest evergreen content an online marketer can produce is a guide or cheat sheet. In fact, sometimes it seems so simple, it is difficult to believe that customers would actually respond to it. However, if it's done well, and with authority, it can provide long lasting lead generation, product demonstrations, recruit enticement, and even image re-alignment.

Examples

• Photographer- The Five Things I Always Have in My Camera Bag

• Outdoor/Camping Outfitter- Top Ten Tools Every Survival Kit Needs

• Author- Teacher's Guide to (Your Book Title)

• Dentist- How I Got My Kids to Brush Their Teeth

YouTube Videos

You don't have to have an expensive Hollywood sound stage or a cutting edge recording studio to produce an elegant and useful YouTube video. In fact, you don't have to start with a video at all. You can start with images, photographs, or even screenshots and blend them together into an integrated video complete with music and professional looking transitions. Of course, if you have the staff or resources to afford a professional camera crew, that will work too. Just make sure it reflects the message you are trying to portray.

YouTube videos make outstanding How-To's for everything from using software to arts and crafts. As long as the topic is in line with your brand, it can be a useful piece of content for your marketing.

Examples:

- Software Developer- How to use X-feature on Y-Program 2.1

- Antique Dealer- How to refinish a solid oak table

- Orchard Manager- How to bake an apple pie

- Author- Book trailer

Podcast

A podcast is an audio or an audiovisual program made available to download over the internet. Podcasts are similar to blogs in that they have an ongoing requirement to perform on a regular basis. If you aren't going to commit to doing at least one podcast every week or two weeks, then you might as well just create a few evergreen YouTube videos and be done with it.

Webinar

On the other hand, a seminar on the web, i.e. a webinar, can be an excellent way to engage with current or potential clients. They can generate leads, prove authority, demonstrate a product, and get customer feedback. Even five to ten years ago, if you wanted to communicate with a room full of people, the cost in time and resources was astronomical. Now you can do the same thing from your home.

Steps for Webinar Proficiency

- Determine the topic that best meets the needs of your company and campaign.

- Set up a scheduled time to host the webinar.

- Start sending out invitations to your e-mail list and social media contacts.

- Engage a webinar hosting service.

- At the appointed time, sign in, make your introduction and share your screens with your audience.

- Proceed to give your talk just like you would if you were in a meeting or giving a seminar.

- Keep the audience engaged by giving shout-outs to people who respond to questions online.

- Allow audience members to type in their questions during the webinar.

- Record the webinar to use as evergreen content for the future.

- Send copies of the recording and your slides to attendees.

- For those who signed up, but could not attend, e-mail a copy of the recording and slides with a limited time for them to access.

- Retain the content to use for future lead magnets and other evergreen content.

Classes/Courses

Classes usually use the same technology as the webinar, however, there are some significant differences and reasons to use a class, instead of a webinar.

• A class may teach someone about something they already own so they will continue to be satisfied with the product, and to help them engage more fully.

• A class may teach about something they want or need, so they will become more emotionally invested in the product or service.

• A class may be conducted over some weeks, instead of just one seminar like a webinar.

• Classes are more costly to perform, and usually require more time, so make sure you are getting a good ROI if you decide to proceed.

Templates

These can be an inexpensive and easy-to-develop form of evergreen content that is often much appreciated by customers. Templates are pre-formatted documents that customers can use to fill in the blanks and customize for their own needs. They make great lead magnets, especially in service related businesses. They also perform very well on SEO.

Examples

• Publishers- e-book templates and cover design templates

• Lawyers- living will templates, asset splitting templates

• Job Sites/HR Recruiters- resume templates

Infographics

Infographics are now the darlings of content marketing. It seems like everyone is racing to put out these visual gems.

And why not? Consumers love them. If a picture is worth a 1000 words, a good infographic is worth 10,000. They perform well across the board. They provide the visual content the social media sites crave. They thrill the pants off Google Analytics. And to top it off, they're insanely fun to create.

Steps for Infographic Proficiency

- Plan your copy to keep your content short and sweet.

- Use a template that fits your message.

- Make sure it looks clean, uncluttered, and easy to follow.

- Don't be afraid to be a bit playful with this medium.

- Make sure it's optimized for mobile devices.

Slides

Your PowerPoint slides may be a side benefit attached to a webinar, or might act as evergreen content on their own. They can serve some of the same functions as an infographic or a video by providing an extremely visual form of content. They can also be maintained on an evergreen basis which makes them an excellent value. Especially if they were originally developed to accompany some other form of content, such as a webinar.

Steps for Slide Proficiency

- Plan your content to make sure your message is clear, and on point.

- Keep your copy direct and uncluttered, use the visuals to tell the story.

- If you used the slides in-house, or for another presentation, make sure they are entirely relevant before repackaging them for content marketing.

- Make sure they are up to date.

- Make sure they are optimized for mobile devices.

White Papers

White papers have started to get so much attention and focus from marketers that they are becoming decidedly gray. Once a British term for a government document, the term "white paper," has loosely come to mean a report that carries authority and provides concise information about a broad problem. They are often seen as the go-to form of media where a sense of convention is desired. They are widely used by professionals of every ilk to convey a sense of authority with their stark appearance and formal text.

White papers perform very well on SEO, especially if appropriate care has been taken to incorporate relevant keywords. They have an evergreen quality that makes them attractive from a cost perspective, but they must be kept up to date. Creating a white paper that provides information, in an attempt to sell a product, without appearing to sell a product is a delicate balance. If the document reads as too "salesy" it can damage the reputation of the company. Drawing that fine line requires a finesse that not every writer is up to.

Steps for White Paper Proficiency

- If you don't have someone on your team that can produce a well-vetted white paper, hire a freelancer. Again, your social media agency should be able to provide one.

• Make sure the person is familiar with your position, values, and organizational objectives.

• Make sure the content is kept up to date.

• Make sure the content is clear and concise, with an informative tone, not a pitch.

Coupons

Last but not least in the content marketing spectrum are coupons. These are a great way to generate leads, increase social media authority, drive sales, and promote time-constrained goals. They cost next to nothing to produce, and they only cost the company when they are used to purchase a product.

You just need to be aware of how the coupons will affect your bottom line. They don't perform as well on SEO, unless people are specifically searching for one of your coupons, and they don't make good evergreen content, but for product marketers especially, they are an excellent tool.

TYPES OF MARKETING CAMPAIGNS

The next step is formulating a goal for your marketing campaigns that add the specificity and time constraints that make them actually measurable, and allow you to analyze your results. There are three basic campaign parameters:

- Ongoing

- Limited Time

- Specific Target

Ongoing campaigns

Use evergreen content marketing to engage people with your business. They might also use serialized, weekly, daily, or bi-weekly content to create a dialog with visitors.

This type of campaign is not bound by an end date, it carries on month after month. However, because it's not time bound, it needs to be monitored on a regular basis to evaluate its ongoing efficacy.

Adjustments need to be made to respond to changing circumstances and to react to your target's feedback and engagement.

Goal: Generate Views and Traffic to Your Company's Website

Example: Millennial Investing has a weekly blog. Every Friday, they list the top ten highest-performing stocks for the week and provide an analysis of why each one did well. They call it "Free Tip Friday," or "FTF."

This is an example of providing valuable information that social advocates can get excited about. They can feel proud to share this type of information with their network of people who have a common interest in investing.

It's also the kind of benefit search engines like Google love.

It's an ongoing campaign because every Friday, without fail, someone in the organization is going to post this blog. It's on the editorial calendar. The person responsible has a back-up and the back-up has a back-up.

Investors come to depend on this blog and assign authority and relevance to Millennial Investing as a result.

Goal: Demonstrate Features

Example: Graphic is a software company that specializes in do-it-yourself graphic design, and it has an "Online University." It consists of a set of videos that demonstrate how to use the product. However, it goes beyond that. It introduces people of all skill levels to the essential tools of graphic design.

The videos start out basic, and progress through higher levels of difficulty.

They are interactive so the user can practice while going through the tutorial.

As new products are added, new tutorials are created to introduce users to the new skills.

People all over the world now have access to simple graphic design tools, and are able to share their creations across all of their social networks. When the people in their network ask them how they learned to make such stunning graphics, they point them back to Graphic.

Goal: Make Customer Service Results Transparent

Example: GeekTeam is a hardware support provider that provides online support for any type of computer hardware. Customers can open a support ticket by Instant Message, through Facebook, via Tweet on Twitter, through a post on Pinterest, or on Skype.

The goal of GeekTeam is to respond to customer inquiries 24/7, within 20 minutes of receiving a message through any of its online platforms.

They want all of their customer support and service interactions to be visible to anyone, with a definite time stamp for each communication and resolution.

They encourage customers to rate their experience at the end of each interaction.

They have a microsite embedded in their website that runs a constant stream of customer service interactions from all of the platforms.

If a potential client wants to see what type of response and turn around they can expect, they can access the "Ongoing Support" tab from the GeekTeam website and watch live transactions.

Also, a potential customer can type in their question or problem in a search query, and see how the situation was handled for another client.

Limited Time Campaigns

Obviously, limited time campaigns are designed to be conducted over a set period of time, and linked to measurable goals once the time frame has concluded. If they are successful, they can always be repeated, or they may involve content that changes once the campaign is completed.

Goal: 120 Day Campaign to Increase Search Engine Rank by Using Keywords

Example: Bree Picta is a Portrait Photographer. She wants to increase her search engine rank over the next 120 days. Her current rank when searching for baby photos is #8 and she intends to move up to #3.

She improves all of the title metadata for each page of her site

She expands the description metadata to include her address, phone number, and hours of operation, along with a Google maps locator.

She includes the keywords: baby photos, baby photographer, pictures of newborn babies, newborn baby portraits, and babies in pictures.

She includes sample pictures from each of her photo sessions on her "looks" page. For each picture, she has rich alt tags.

She has links to Facebook, Twitter, Instagram, and Pinterest.

Bree also has a "Lead Magnet" called "5 Steps to Fabulous Baby Pictures." It's her top five tips for taking great baby pictures. She sends it out whenever someone signs up for her e-mail list.

Goal: A university wants to increase its enrollment by improving its Net Promoter Score between September and April.

They host a series of webinars for potential students, they host webinars for parents of potential applicants, and they host webinars for both parents and students together.

During the webinar, they show a 20-minute video made by the student videography team that shows various aspects of campus life. They have several messages based on the audience, but all designed to drive interest in attending the University.

During the webinar, participants are encouraged to ask questions, and the questions are shared with the audience.

Following the webinar, all of the questions are compiled and sent out as a Q&A document to all participants, along with the slides and other information.

After the webinar, applicants are contacted by a current student who spends time answering any questions, and getting their feedback about the university through a series of survey questions.

Specific Target

This type of campaign is more focused on a particular goal than the time it takes to accomplish the goal. However, it still has to be completed in an amount of time considered reasonable for its execution. It also should be monitored to make sure it is effective in achieving the particular goal.

Goal: Launch on a new social media platform and get X number of users within the first 90 days.

In this case, the goal is more about ramping up to a certain number of users on a new platform than the time frame.

Example: The zoo has decided to start using Pinterest to market to mothers with children four-to-eight years old.

They want to increase their followers from 500 to 5000 over the next 30 days.

They create a Zoo Page with multiple boards.

Baby Animals- for pictures of the baby animals at the zoo.

Penguins- for photos in the penguin exhibit.

All Animals- For pictures of any of the animals.

Fun Times- For pictures of people having fun at the zoo.

Photo Club Members- For pictures taken by the photo club.

When people post their pictures from the zoo on the zoo Facebook or Twitter sites, the Social Media Manager makes sure they are included on the Pinterest page.

They enlist the help of the volunteer "Photo Club" to post their pictures.

They encourage other staff and volunteers to take photos and videos and post them on social media and Pinterest.

Goal: Launch a Campaign to Generate Resumes

StarTrack is a virtual call center looking to hire the best agents worldwide. Their specific goal is to have a steady stream of reliable, efficient, multi-cultural agents available at all times. These people will work from home, so they have to be able to work independently. StarTrack prides itself on having the most helpful and empathetic agents of any business. They empower their employees to make decisions independently with little supervision.

They use the power of social media to attract potential agents. They start by using LinkedIn to target a group of possible candidates for their initial pool.

They also use Twitter, Facebook, and Google+ to broadcast to other targets.

They host a weekly webinar that highlights the benefits or working for StarTrack. Applicants never have to pay anything to participate in any way. The webinar outlines the selection process, which is rigorous. This weeds out the uncommitted and challenges those who are very interested.

After they have hired a pool of qualified agents, they keep their campaign progressing by giving their employees incentives for sharing the message on social media. Working associates receive bonuses for recruiting other qualified individuals through LinkedIn, Twitter, Facebook, or any social platform.

The goal of your campaign might be an ongoing result, a time-bound outcome, or a particular target. In some cases, it might combine parts of all three. You may have a particular goal that is managed on an ongoing basis with specific timed milestones to vouch for accomplishment. You might have a time-bound campaign that is repeated on a continuous basis for concrete results.

DEVELOP YOUR CAMPAIGN

So far we've discussed the underlying elements that go into creating a successful social media campaign. It starts with having the right components. The correct blend of search engine optimization and marketing, and content marketing supported by social media outreach. Next is to identify the desired outcomes of the campaign to ensure you know what success looks like. What are your goals? Do you want to generate leads, increase your social authority, demonstrate your product, unveil your customer service, and alter how you are perceived, or recruit new employees? Finally, what structure is required to support your campaign? Should it be ongoing, or time-bound? Are your goals specific or general?

Once you have this foundation, the next step is to build and execute your particular campaign. There are three broad steps that need to be taken. Each of these steps may have multiple levels beneath it.

Planning

- Who are primary, secondary, tertiary, and other target audiences?

- What are the unique selling propositions?

- Which combination of Social Media, SEO, SEM and Content Marketing is needed?

- Select Social Media, SEO, SEM and Content Marketing platforms.

- Select Social Media accounts: company, employee, personal, customer, or influencer.

• Determine content needed for each platform and develop timetable for content.

Finalize schedule and content for each platform knowing social accounts are linked

• When do you want to reach your targets?

• If you have linked your social media accounts, your schedule needs to factor that in.

• If your Twitter, Facebook, and Instagram accounts are linked, when you post on Instagram, Twitter can send out a tweet of your post, and it can also be posted on Facebook.

• If you're using one of the management tools we discuss in Chapter 7, this can be automated for you.

Execution

• Make sure that you are executing your schedule on a daily basis.

• Spelling, grammar, content and timing need to be 100% every time.

Analysis

• Measure results regularly

• Post-mortem at end of campaign to document lessons learned for future

• Define goals for next campaign

After reviewing these steps, we will be creating some Campaign Studies to illustrate how each phase of the process works together.

PLANNING

Identify your primary, secondary, tertiary, and other target audiences.

Primary Target Audience- This is the person who you created your product or service for in the first place. It's that person you've had in your mind through every phase of development. Now it's time to get out your BUYER DESCRIPTION and start filling in the blanks. What does your ideal buyer look like?

Secondary Target Audience- This is someone who is very similar to your primary target audience, but may have one or two key differences. How is this person unique, and what special tweaks do you need to make to reach and enlist this audience? Create a BUYER DESCRIPTION for your secondary target.

Tertiary Target Audience- This is the third group of people who make up your target audience. They are less likely to become a partner than your first and second targets, but with the right campaign, can become engaged. Create a BUYER DESCRIPTION for your tertiary goal.

Quaternary or Other Target Audience- This is the fourth group of people who make up your target audience, and anyone beyond a fourth group. These are people that get swept up into the campaign as a residual effect of targeting your primary and secondary audience. These people who might not see themselves as a potential partner, but under the right circumstances would be a good potential target. Create a BUYER DESCRIPTION for your quaternary target(s).

Creating a tangible worksheet is key here. Even down to having a picture of the person. The more closely you can relate to an individual target for your campaign, the more likely you are to captivate your audience. These worksheets should be shared with your whole company, and the targets should be discussed like they are real people. When you meet to analyze your progress, don't say, "How are our Primary Target's doing?" instead say, "How is Sharon Clark doing?"

What are the unique selling propositions?

What is unique about your product or service? What makes it stand out from the competition? Really think about the word unique. It gets thrown around a lot to describe things that are different, but unique is more than different. Unique is one-of-a-kind. So what makes your product or service one-of-a-kind, like no other?

First make sure everyone in your company knows why you are unique. Then include this in your plans for engaging your network of loyal partners.

Which combination of Social Media, SEO, SEM and Content Marketing is needed?

This is where you need to analyze your goals, and the type of campaign you feel is necessary to achieve the desired outcomes.

Budget- what is your budget for this endeavor? How much can you afford to spend? What are the opportunity costs of spending too little? Your budget will determine, in part, what you can afford to spend developing content, and paying for search engine marketing in the form of pay per click advertising and PPC on the social media channels.

Time frame- do you have a necessary time frame for this campaign, or is this going to be an ongoing strategy? If it's ongoing, what milestones will you use to indicate success? Some tactics and combinations will have a more immediate outcome, while others will garner long-term results. Understanding your desired outcomes is important.

Personnel- who do you have in place to manage the campaign? Do you have people who can create the content required or do you need to outsource? What about search engine optimization; is your site and your content fully optimized? Do you have an SEO czar within the company that establishes policy and monitors optimization? If not, have you taken the time to enlist the help of a social media agency? Who do you need to make all the pieces of the puzzle come together?

Outcomes- what does success look like for this campaign? If you want to generate more leads, how many? If you want to recruit new employees, who are your targets? If you want to change your image, what feedback on social media will mean you have succeeded?

Existing infrastructure- what tools do you already have in place to support your campaign? Is your SEO in impeccable shape, but your social media platforms are weak or non-existent? Do you need to create additional content to support a particular goal or appeal to a primary target? Or do you already have great content that may just need some tweaking?

Plan B

No one wants to need a B or C plan. You plan to use your A game from the outset. But organizations who don't have secondary and tertiary plans in place are poorly positioned to respond if their primary plan doesn't work out as planned. Before you proceed to execution, make sure you have a backup plan, and a back-up to your back-up. That way, if your campaign doesn't turn out the way you expected, you have secondary and tertiary plans in place that can be deployed quickly.

Or perhaps you've decided to use an A/B Split to determine the effectiveness of your content. Is the ABC or XYZ more engrossing? Do people prefer a yellow call to action button, or is red better? Does your target audience respond more favorably to a two-week time limit or a fourteen-day trial? If you have A, B, and C choices set up for your content before you start your campaign, you can make changes on the fly without losing any valuable momentum.

Select social media, SEO, SEM, and content marketing platforms

Now you have a clear picture of the resources you can bring to the campaign and the outcomes you require to be successful. It's just a matter of selecting the right combination of social media, SEO/SEM, and content marketing to support your campaign. In the next chapter, we will discuss the merits of the major social media platforms. Keep in mind, you will be more successful by integrating several platforms that each contribute to the campaign.

Select Social Media accounts: company, employee, personal, customer, and influencer

Once you have determined which social media outlets are appropriate for your campaign, you need to determine which you have in place, and where you need to add or alter them.

Company- do you have company accounts that reflect the spirit of the campaign and can be used, or do you need to add accounts? If you add accounts, how will you incorporate them into your existing accounts to take advantage of the foundation you have in place? If this is a service campaign, add a separate service social media account.

Employee- do your employees have social media accounts that can be used to benefit your campaign? If so, are there any limitations you need to put in place for your employees?

How will your employees know what to post and when to post it? What parameters will you need to ensure that employees are using their personal accounts to promote the message of the campaign, and not going off-script and damaging your efforts?

Personal- does your leadership team have personal accounts that can enhance the message of your campaign and promote engagement with customers? If not, perhaps you should consider campaigns for your leadership to establish them as thought leaders in your industry.

Customer- do you have existing customers that act as supporters? Can they be counted on to broadcast your message organically, or do they need to be directed?

Influencers- are there any influential people in your industry that can be relied on to support your campaign? Do you know any experts in your field that will endorse your message? Do you have a symbiotic relationship with any organization that can act as an influencer? Do you need to have your social media agency help with influencer marketing?

Determine content needed for each platform and develop a timetable for content completion and distribution.

Now that you know what social media platforms you will be using, you can establish the right mix of content for each and determine a strategy for when it will be implemented. You need to create a content calendar for the lifetime of the campaign.

Based on your primary, secondary, and tertiary target audience, determine what time they are most likely to engage with each platform. Set up your content calendar to deploy your campaign at the peak time for each target to see it, and absorb it.

Finalize schedule and content for each platform knowing social accounts are linked

You're almost ready to pull the trigger on your campaign, but before you do, you should test everything to make sure it works the way you anticipated. There is nothing that will undermine your credibility faster than having a poorly functioning campaign. Make sure you do a final check to ensure everything is linked and working the way you want.

Make any necessary changes to produce the desired outcome before you flip the switch. Make sure to allow yourself enough time to restructure or redevelop before the deployment. If you don't have enough time to fix problems, then you will be forced to move your timeline back. This could end up causing you to lose a vital window of opportunity.

Execute your campaign

Most people think this is the most important part of the campaign. The moment when you actually implement your strategy. It is certainly where you're going to see your campaign in action. And obviously, if you never deploy the campaign, you are never going to see any results. But if you have set up everything correctly, this should be the easiest part of the process.

At this stage, you should have a robust content calendar full of tools that have been tested and automated. During the execution phase, they need to be monitored to ensure that no glitches have been introduced that could cause them to fail or perform below expectation.

Measure results regularly

Whether you have an ongoing campaign or a time-bound campaign, you need to measure results on a regular basis.

Analyzing outcomes should be included on your content calendar and assigned to a specific person. Each social media platform has tools available to analyze performance. Google Analytics is a great way to evaluate the success of your campaign. At given intervals, you need to determine if your goals being achieved. If not, put Plan B in place and evaluate its effectiveness.

Post-mortem at end of campaign to document lessons learned for future

This is probably the step that organizations most often skip at their own peril. If you skip this step and move to quickly into another campaign, you forfeit the ability to learn from both your mistakes and your successes.

To be truly successful, a campaign needs to be followed up by a thorough evaluation of each tool to determine how well each one performed, even if it was an undeniable success. Look at each element of your campaign to see how well each piece did against expectations. Did any one factor stand out far above the others, if so why? Was there a weak link that could have been strengthened? A thorough examination of the campaign will put you much farther ahead in developing your next campaign.

Define goals for next campaign

Now that you've evaluated your previous campaign, you're ready to start defining the goals for your next campaign. You're in a great position to determine what went well, and what needs to be altered next time. You can build on your past results to create Specific, Measurable, Achievable, Relevant and Time-bound goals.

Now that you know all the steps to creating an effective campaign let's look at a sample that puts everything together.

SAMPLE CAMPAIGN: Umea Furniture

Overview:

Umea Furniture is an international furniture company that is known for its innovation in design, its affordability, and its use of technology. They have developed a line of multipurpose furniture called the MinMax line.

The first product is a coffee table that has a pivoting top that can be raised and extended to become a dining table. It can also be raised to become a workstation. The base can be used for storage. It is built on lockable casters that allow it to be moved anywhere in the room. The top can be rotated to reveal a cushioned surface that turns the table into a seat for two people.

Define primary, secondary, tertiary, and other target audiences

Primary Target: Penny Young-Professional

Background

Penny is a young professional who recently graduated college and is moving into her first apartment. She just got her first job at a NY City Publishing House.

Demographics

- Female

- 24-35

- Single

- No Children

- Income $36,000 per year

- Urban

Identifiers

- Very tuned into social media and its uses for publishing.

- Concerned that publishing is falling behind and hopes to be a force for change and an example of her generation.

- Detail-orientated and rabid about grammar and punctuation.

- Not only loves to read but has to read for work.

- Commutes to work, but hoping to prove reliable so she can work from home.

- Likes to cook and throw small dinner parties.

Goals

- Get an editorial position, hopes to have her own imprint someday.

- Wants to be able to work from home to save the commute from Brooklyn.

- Hoping to marry her boyfriend and settle down in the next five years.

Challenges

- Finding space to work in her apartment.

- Boyfriend is unreliable.

What can Umea do?

Provide her a space saving solution that can function as a desk and storage unit for her home office equipment when she's working. It can be a coffee table while she's reading books, and a table when she wants to have people over for dinner.

Objections

- Affordability

- Ease of use

Secondary Target: Tim Tiny home

Overview

Tim is a middle-aged history teacher who has had it with teaching public school kids and decided to realize his dream of writing the ultimate Revolutionary War novel. He took early retirement from the school district.

Demographics

- Male

- Age 45-60

- Divorced

- Grown Children

- Identifiers

Identifiers

- Slightly reclusive, introvert

- Above average education and intelligence

- Intellectual

Goals

- He sold his condo and is downsizing to a tiny house of only 168 square feet.

- He plans to build his house, and live off the grid, mortgage free, traveling between the State and National Parks of the East Coast.

- He wants to research his "Great American Novel" and then write it. He wants to live as economically as possible, so he doesn't use all his retirement savings before he reaches 65.

Challenges

- Finding storage space for books and research materials, as well as all his other necessities in a tiny home.

- Having a place to work in his 168 square foot home.

What Umea can do?

Provide a multifunctioning piece of furniture that will fit into the tiny home and act like a desk, coffee table, storage and dining.

Objections

Space required.

What are the unique selling propositions?

- Multifunction- The piece serves as a coffee table, a dining table, a workstation/surface, seating, and storage.

- Ease of use- The hinged top lifts up easily to form a perfectly elevated work surface that can be used as a desk or table for one. The top then folds over to expand the table surface to seat four to six. Or the top can be flipped over to provide a cushioned surface that acts as a bench. Below the top is a storage container with slide out drawers.

• All of the mechanisms are lightweight and easy to operate.

• The castors on the bottom lock in place when it is stationary, but can roll when needed, making it easy to move.

Select Social Media, SEO, SEM and Content Marketing platforms

• Content Marketing

• The company makes a long format demo video showing all of the functions of the table.

• They cut out a short format video that plays well on Twitter, Facebook, and Pinterest.

• They create an additional Lead Magnet called "Top Ten Ways to Make the Most of a Small Space." At the top of the list is using multipurpose furniture.

• They develop a weekly newsletter called "Small Space Solutions." Each week they highlight an elegantly furnished small space. Their furniture usually features prominently in the newsletter. They use a good balance of keywords to improve their SEO ranking.

• Being featured in the newsletter is highly desirable for interior decorators who readily provide photos of their work. The photos all have rich "Alt" text descriptions.

• They use the Lead Magnet to gather e-mail subscribers for their newsletter.

• The newsletter has buttons that allow readers to forward the content to Twitter, Facebook, Pinterest, Instagram, and Google+.

• SEO/SEM

• The set up a microsite, embedded in their main website. The microsite specifically deals with the MinMax line of furniture.

• They optimize their web page with clear Meta description tags. They actually developed two different tags and will A/B Test them to see which one gets the best results.

• They added an XML Sitemap as well as an image sitemap.

• They purchased advertising on Google AdWords. Because they included a rich description and other searchable information about the address, phone, and hours of their stores by location, they are rewarded with a high ranking at a reasonable rate.

Social Media

• Umea has been active on social media for over ten years now and has established a robust following on Facebook, Twitter, Pinterest, Instagram, Google+, and YouTube. They use each of these outlets effectively. They establish individual accounts for the MinMax brand and link them to their Umea accounts.

• They have been encouraging their staff members to use social media to promote the company for years. They have a clear-cut policy on what is acceptable and what is not when using social media to promote the company. Many associates have social media accounts specifically for cross-promoting Umea.

• They have been engaging the Interior Design Community for years to help cross-promote their products. They give extra discounts and other benefits to designers who not only use their furniture, but link back to Umea in their blogs and websites.

Plan B

• Each part of the campaign has a secondary and tertiary option. They will use A/B Split Testing throughout the campaign to see which elements get the best responses, and carry on with those.

• The newsletter campaign has a secondary plan of doing a webinar series instead. This will be much more costly, but might be the only choice if the newsletter doesn't elicit the response they are hoping for.

• They have six different lead magnets to try, including an online magazine from some of their top designers. They would prefer to save this tool for future product offerings, however, and hope the "Top Ten List" will generate the leads they need.

• Their most famous designer has agreed to write one of their newsletters. They are going to wait until they see a dip in the lead generation before they issue that very special newsletter.

SMART Goal

• They want to establish a list of 40,000 leads over the first 90 days after implementation.

Determine content needed for each platform and develop timetable

They build a content calendar for the overall campaign.

	Mon	Tues	Wed	Thur	Fri	Sat	Sun
Newsletter		9:00AM					
Facebook				1:00PM	3:00PM		
Twitter			12:00PM	12:00PM	12:00PM	6:00PM	6:00PM
Pinterest						10:00 PM	
Instagram	3:00PM						
Google+	10:00AM	10:00AM	10:00AM				

Finalize schedule and content for each platform knowing social accounts are linked

They tested everything over a two week time period before rolling it out to their network.

Measure results regularly

- They deployed the campaign and have a follow-up schedule as follows. Day 1, day 7, day 14, day 28, day 56, day 90.

- At day 14 they noticed that the Pinterest site is performing well above what was anticipated, and they add Pins on Sunday, Tuesday and Thursday at 2:00 AM. Google+ is not performing as well as anticipated. They split test adding a post at 2:00 PM Tues-Thur.

- At day 28 all of the sites are doing well, they have 26,879 leads, which is way ahead of their goal run rate.

- At day 56 they have 38,212 leads and look to be on track to reach their goal. However, lead generation has fallen behind the pace set over the first 28 days of deployment. Click through rates have fallen off on all of the major social networks. They realize they need something to generate more buzz. They have been saving a newsletter post from the most famous Interior Decorator they work with. She is planning to feature the MinMax in a design she's working on for a celebrity client. Umea feels this should generate enough leads to get them to the finish line.

Post-mortem at end of campaign to document lessons learned for future

• At day 90 they reviewed the success of the campaign. In all, they got 66,791 leads, more than 66% over their goal. They feel they did not set their goal high enough. However, now that they have baseline figures, they will know what to expect for the next campaign. They found that the newsletter program worked well and felt it was a big benefit having the celebrity designer involved. They plan to solicit more help from him.

• They feel that the lead magnet they used has served its purpose, and they are ready to use the more robust magazine for the next campaign.

• A whole line of MinMax furniture will be rolling out over the next six months.

• Plan for next campaign

• Based on lessons learned they have come up with a solid plan to ramp up their presence to help support the rollout of a larger line of furniture.

• This is just one campaign study showing how all of the elements of content marketing, SEO/SEM, and social media work together. It's an overall strategy to engage potential clients and help you be seen, be heard, and be memorable.

SOCIAL MEDIA PLATFORMS

Twitter

Twitter is also known as a microblog. Users are limited to 140 characters per "tweet," similar to sending a text message. It was started in 2006, and has over 500 million users. Currently they rank #9 worldwide on Alexa and #8 in the US. Tweets are visible to the user's followers or "tweeps."

Some of the first active users on Twitter were celebrities or their promotional staff. They could quickly give 140 character views into their daily life. Their fans were able to feel connected by knowing what Ashton Kutcher had for lunch, or which pair of shoes Paris Hilton was going to wear tonight.

Soon everyone was providing 140 character glimpses into their daily lives. It didn't take long for savvy businesses to realize that they needed a Twitter presence to remain relevant and maintain authority in their field. But just having a Twitter account, and thousands or even millions of followers, won't do any good if you're not sending relevant and consistent tweets.

Part of the challenge of Twitter is the sheer volume of tweets that most users receive on a minute-by-minute basis. Anyone who is active on Twitter will likely be following several thousand users at least. For the average user, following is a two-way street. People often follow you if you follow them. Therefore, if you want more followers, you have to follow more people.

For businesses, this is not necessarily the case. Individuals may follow a Fortune 500 company, knowing that they will never be followed back. A celebrity may have 7 million followers and only follow 375. However, for the vast majority of people actively using the service, they are following thousands, if not tens of thousands of people. This can make it very difficult to hear any one person's particular message.

Companies differentiate themselves by using Hashtags #. If the pound sign (#), or hashtag precedes a word, all tweets concerning that #word are grouped together. For example, let's say you are a potential customer who wants to know what people are saying about the MinMax furniture line from Umea. They have established the hashtag, #MinMax for people to ask questions and give feedback. They have a staffer that responds in real-time 24/7. All you have to do is search for #MinMax and you can see the stream of tweets about the product.

If a person wants to save a tweet so they can refer to it again in the future, they use the "favorite," feature. This adds it to a list that they can access at any time in the future. Twitter users can also "pin" a tweet to the top of their list. This makes it possible to put their most important message at the top of their feed, where it's easy for followers to find it.

Tweeters can also "retweet" tweets that other people have sent. This gives people the ability to have things to tweet about, without coming up with their own content. It's also a great way for people to share things that they think will have value to their followers. Further, it is appreciated by the original tweeter, who may reciprocate by retweeting something of theirs. (That's where those handy "pinned" tweets come in. Someone who wants to retweet something for you can just pick your top tweet.)

Businesses are using Twitter for some applications. But to be effective, businesses have to think beyond just advertising. People don't like ads, and when they have the chance, they avoid them. Businesses that do nothing but push products and services will have few followers. Instead, businesses have to offer something worth listening to. Information, service, solutions, and humor are all things that customers value, and reasons that they will follow an organization.

The more information is available, the more people seem to want. Now it's possible to get accurate answers to any question you can think of from your computer or your phone. That's the kind of information people want to possess. Companies that supply information as a way to establish a relationship with a customer can gain traction on Twitter.

Another opportunity is providing service to customers. Twitter is a great place for people to vent their frustrations about companies, products, or services, and they do. No company wants to see a lot of complaints about them on their Twitter feed. But it happens, and it can damage your reputation. But it can also be a chance to look like a hero.

Currently, less than 30% of all companies are taking the time to respond when a customer complains on Twitter. This is a huge missed opportunity, and it takes your company out of the equation when it comes to your online reputation. And if @yourcompanyname is used preceded by a # or @ then that complaint, and more importantly, your lack of response to it is out there on Twitter for anyone to see.

On the other hand, you have the opportunity to respond to the complaint in a way that makes it clear that you value customer service and take a proactive role in resolving issues. You can even go one further and encourage and support the use of Twitter for providing customer service. Similar to having online support, you can use Twitter as your vehicle for solving customer issues.

If it's done well, this can give your company a transparency when it comes to providing service that can establish your reputation and authority as a service-centric organization. Of course, this takes dedicated management. People are using Twitter around the clock, and things move very fast. If you don't have the staff to support this type of endeavor, you should not consider it.

However, even a small staff can make a daily habit of searching for your company online to see what people are saying, and then responding when necessary. Since over 70% of your competition is not doing this, it's an easy way to get ahead.

Facebook

Facebook is by far the largest social media network in the world with over 1.2 billion users worldwide and growing (although they are banned in China). The company was started in 2004 by Mark Zuckerberg in his Harvard dorm room and currently has an Alexa rank is #2, second only to Google.

Facebook is a social networking application that allows people, groups, or businesses to post things about themselves, their group, or their organization. You can allow access to your information by permitting someone to become your "Friend." Only friends can see your personal information, unless you choose to make it public to all.

However, if you have a business, you can create one of six different types of Facebook Business Pages

• Local Business or Place- This is for people with a brick and mortar storefront that they want people to come visit. Even if you also sell things online, if you have a physical building this is the best type of page for you.

- Company Business or Location- If your business doesn't have a physical location, or if you have many different locations this is the option for you.

- Brand or Product- If your products are sold through more than one website, or sold through multiple retailers then you want a Brand/Product page.

- Artist, Band, or Public Figure- If your page is focused on promoting you, then this is the kind of page you would choose.

- Entertainment Page- If your business is part of the entertainment industry such as an album, concert, movie, TV show, book, play, etc. then this is the page you need.

- Cause or Community- This can be used for non-profit organizations or civic organizations like cities, towns, etc.

You can also create groups on Facebook to bring a specific group of people together. These can be used internally for teams of people within your organization, or for people outside your organization. They can be private, invitation-only groups, or groups that anyone can join.

It goes without saying that on a platform that has over 1.2 billion users, it is pretty much required that you have a Facebook page for your business. If nothing else, to prove your relevance. Even the least tech savvy people would wonder why a company doesn't have a Facebook page. But if you're not using your Facebook page as a way to engage with your audience, you're missing out on a golden opportunity. Besides, many other forms of advertising are becoming irrelevant. When was the last time you looked at the Yellow Pages? Have you ever fast forwarded through commercials? How often do you read the newspaper? Yet, businesses advertising on Facebook are getting excellent results. And even if you're not paying for advertising, you still need to have an active presence.

If you're convinced that you need to start advertising on Facebook, what outcomes are you looking for? Do you want to create a following by increasing the number of Likes? Or do you want to send people to your web page to make a purchase? Each of these options has benefits, and maybe a combination of both would be best.

Attracting Likes is ideal for a business that wants people to come to them, rather than buying online. Restaurants and bars, beauty shops, spas, movie theaters, entertainment venues, anyone that doesn't have a product that they can sell online.

Likes are important for more than just a straight popularity contest. Likes tell you what other people you know, respect, or aspire to emulate care about. Let's say you're trying to choose between two popular new dinner spots. You've never been to either. You go to their Facebook pages to get their hours and an idea of their menu. You see on one page that three of your good friends have "Liked" the page. Everything else being equal, their preference would be a good reason for choosing that restaurant.

Purchase Links are better for businesses who are interested in driving online sales, but don't have the resources to focus a lot on their Facebook page.

A combination might work best where you can also set up your advertising to have people Like your page before they are taken to your website. Although this makes another click-through necessary, it can be beneficial in promoting your brand.

Targeted Ads

Facebook has the ability to identify your target market and allow you to advertise to those people. This is not necessarily revolutionary. Print and broadcast media have long targeted their advertising to different market segments. Facebook can do the same thing, with even more precision and focus than most print or broadcast media could attain. They do this by taking the same information we used for our customer profile and using it to set up the ideal ad.

Location

> • You can specify anything from as broad as a whole country, or as narrow as a ten-block radius of your business.
>
> • If your business is brick and mortar, and has very little competition in your local area, you might want to target anyone in your zip code or even your city.
>
> • If your business is a coffee shop, with a competitor on every corner, you might want to focus on your closest neighbors.
>
> • On the other hand, if you do business electronically for a specialty niche, you might be able to target your advertisement to the whole country.

Demographics

You can target your audience by a long and complex web of demographics that can pinpoint all of the basic demographics like gender and age.

> • Language- What language does your ideal buyer speak?
>
> • Relationship Status- If your product/service is geared toward someone in a specific relationship demographic you can pinpoint if they are looking for a partner (and

specify the particulars) or if they are in a relationship. That way you don't waste your time and money marketing your wedding planning service to someone who has been married for ten years.

• Education- If your business is geared toward someone at a certain level of education, you can target that.

• Work- Are you targeting people who work from home? You can specify that here. Maybe your campaign is designed to recruit new employees and you plan to target your competition's employees, you can specify a certain company and much more. You can also choose what type of work they do.

• Financial- What are your target person's income and net worth? If it's important to your business, you can specify it here.

• Home- Are you targeting renters, homeowners?

• Ethnic Affinity- Is your business geared toward a certain ethnicity? Is there a tie-in that will make it a good fit?

• Generation- Baby boomers, Gen X, Millennial? Very different buying patterns here.

• Parents- This category is broken down into All Parents and Moms. Then they go so far as to specify different types of moms, fit moms, green moms, moms of preschoolers, etc.

• Politics- The US was broken down by party affiliation.

• Life Events- This is fascinating, here they have things like people who are in new jobs, people who are recently engaged, and the list goes on.

— Interests

— In addition to demographics, you can also pinpoint your target's interests.

• Business and Industry- Not necessarily where they work but what they're interested in.

• Entertainment- What do they like to do for entertainment, read, games, movies, etc.

• Family and Relationship- Not do they have them, are they interested in them.

• Fitness and Wellness

• Food and Drink

• Hobbies and Activities

• Shopping and Fashion

• Sports and Outdoors

• Technology

— Behaviors

— You can narrow your targets based on their purchasing behaviors.

• Automotive- Have they recently bought a new car?

• Business to Business- Targeting business owners

• Digital Activities- What have they been doing online?

• Expats- Are they from another country and if so which?

- Charitable Donations- What causes do they support financially?

- Financial- Do they use credit cards, cash, debt?

- Job Role- Management, front line?

- Media- What do they watch on TV, listen to on the radio?

- Mobile Device User?

- Purchase Behavior- What do they spend money on?

- Residential Profile- Have they moved recently, bought a home?

- Seasonal Events- Graduations, Sports Finals

- Travel- Are they a frequent traveler?

— Connections

— Finally, you can narrow your parameters based on the connections they have with other people on Facebook. You can choose not to advertise to people who already like you. Or you can choose to advertise to people who like someone you are close to.

— As you select categories, the system will tell you how many targets you are likely to have. If you make your list too specific, you will either have to pay more to reach those potential targets, or you won't have very many targets. You need to find the right mix by using the Customer Profile you have already built.

LinkedIn

LinkedIn is the Professional to Professional network for business. The site was launched in May of 2003, before either Facebook or Twitter. They have over 380 million users with an Alexa rank of 14. The site is available in 24 languages and is gaining popularity as a social site as well as a business site.

The site allows registered users to publish their business profile online. It is intended to act as a networking platform, and open opportunities for people to network with other professional contacts no matter where they are located.

The personal information on the site is not only demographic in nature, but also delves deep into a person's employment history. This makes it possible for employers to research candidates online, and for candidates to research employers, leadership, and executives.

One of the most obvious ways that companies can use LinkedIn is for recruiting and screening applicants. It is also an excellent tool for promoting your company and the positions available. LinkedIn makes it possible to gather a great deal of information about both applicants and companies.

Another service LinkedIn provides is the ability for users to endorse one another's skills. If a user claims to have a certain skill, another member can verify that they are aware of that skill by endorsing the person.

LinkedIn has an impressive "Influencers Program" with 300 of the worlds leading authorities. People like Richard Branson, Arianna Huffington, Martha Stewart, Deepak Chopra, and Bill Gates share their insights with the LinkedIn community.

One of the most significant factors that differentiate LinkedIn from other social networks is the privacy members receive. On platforms such as Twitter, you can invite anyone to be a follower, whether you know them or not. On Facebook, you can invite "Friends," but they have to accept your invitation. On LinkedIn, though, if you ask to be in someone's network and they turn you down or indicate that they don't know you, then you could be banned from the site.

You have to develop your network through connections with people you do know, to get to the person you want to be in contact with. It is a slow process to build the relationships that will lead to a business on LinkedIn. However, when you have established that relationship, you have a contact that is fully engaged in your success. You just have to be careful to approach people in a very professional manner. Make sure you research them first and make sure you make your approach individual. Don't just fling something at them, hoping that if you get enough on the wall, something will stick.

If you do take a measured and professional approach, it is possible to establish valuable long-term contacts on LinkedIn. However, if you behave irresponsibly, claiming relationships with people that are false, or presuming on weak links, you can severely damage your reputation.

Pinterest

Pinterest is an online image sharing network. It started with a limited beta in 2010 and full application in 2011. They are currently #37 in Alexa rank

The idea behind Pinterest is an online pinboard. In the old days (ten years ago), when you wanted to read content, you primarily went to a magazine or periodical. If you saw a recipe you wanted to try, you cut it out, and perhaps "pinned" it to a corkboard. Same thing goes with a dress, a craft project, or a cute animal. You might share your pinboard with your friends, or make copies of the recipe for them to use. Obviously all this was messy and time consuming.

Now, you can do this all digitally. Instead of having a corkboard in real life that you are pinning cut-out pictures to, you have a digital corkboard. Instead of having to cut them out and pin them up, you just click on them on your computer and add them to a board.

Obviously this has many applications for marketers, especially those that have a physical product to show. It has been especially popular with crafters, who are able to show samples of their crafts. These get shared with their followers, and their followers share with other followers, etc.

Pinterest used to appeal mainly to women, but men have become the fastest growing population on the platform. Sports stats, muscle cars, and DIY are some of the biggest growth segments.

And Pinterest is not just for images. The video is also appreciated. There is a place where you can put a description of your pin, which helps the search engines pick it up. Users are using Pinterest to communicate in writing, by taking images of written content and pinning it. Infographics are another content format that is growing in popularity on Pinterest.

To optimize Pinterest for your business, you need to have relevant images. They don't have to be Annie Leibowitz photographs, they just have to reflect your message. Poems in stylized font can make a striking image that generates a lot of interest. The images are linked to your website, where people can go to find out more about your products.

Interestingly, pinners are very active during the late night, 10:00 p.m.–12:00 a.m. and 2:00 a.m.–4:00 a.m. This may change as the demographic changes. At the outset, when many pinners were women searching for craft ideas, they were probably active after their kids went to bed, or when they couldn't sleep. But as more men enter the platform, the best time to pin may shift. This is something to always keep in mind regarding any social media platform, the rules are always changing.

Another critical feature of Pinterest is to have the "pin it" button on every page and piece of content on your own website. This allows people to pin any of your content to their own boards. This strategy allows you to extend your reach beyond your own Pinterest board and permits engaged partners to share your content on your behalf.

Google +

This is Google's answer to Facebook as a social media outlet. It was started in 2011 to compete for market share with Facebook. They claim to have over a billion followers, and Alexa rank #1, however, this is not differentiated from the total Google platform.

So far Google+ has a very loyal following, especially internationally. They have many of the same features as Facebook, Pinterest, and LinkedIn. They also have some additional features that set them apart and make them an important piece in any social media puzzle.

Google My Business- Well, they aren't called Google+ for nothing. Of course, Google is going to favor their baby over sites like Facebook or LinkedIn. If you take the time to completely fill out your Google+ Business Listing, making sure it is robust and informative, you are sure to be rewarded by the most popular search engine, Google.

Google+ Circles allow you to segment your followers so you can more effectively market to various demographics.

Google+ Communities is one of the ways Google Plus really stands out for businesses. Communities are very engaged and communicative. Just what you need to find to be successful.

Google+ Collections allows you to curate content and segment it for customization across your network.

Google+ Hangouts is one of the coolest features of the platform. It allows you to conference with people all over the world, sharing screens, content, voice, data, and video.

Google+ Pictures- They have by far the most storage available and integrate with maps to enhance the story behind your pictures.

Google+ probably is not ready to stand on its own, and can't take the place of Facebook, but it is an option that can provide a backup, a B Plan, or in some cases a preferred networking option. Once you've attracted engaged followers, it's a way to share extra content with them that can be distributed through their highly interactive circles.

Blogs – Tumblr, WordPress, SquareSpace, etc.

Blogs have been around for a little over fifteen years. They started out as a Web Log, or an online diary, and have evolved into important content outlets for major corporations as well as individual users. Some blogs and bloggers have become so popular that they have become a full-time occupation or even the work of many people. Other blogs are viewed by no one but the blog owner and their relatives.

The shift is definitely moving away from every company, individual, sole proprietorship, and partnership having their own blog. People may just be burned out on blogging, or perhaps they have run out of things to say. There are certain blogs that are still going strong, providing reliable and valuable content. However, if your organization has never had a blog before, and you are just getting into it because, "everyone else is blogging," you should consider waiting.

If you have a legitimate niche that is not being covered by another well-known, heavily followed blog then it might be a good time to start a new blog. Just remember consistency and content are key. They both have to be in full force to make an impact. Blogs are an important part of content marketing campaigns. Outside of campaigns, it's easy to fail if you don't recognize the commitment needed.

There are several popular blog sites available. Some are only capable of managing a blog as a standalone entity. Some are able to operate all functions of a website. On that note, the lines between what is a blog and what is a website can become very gray. A blog is like an online diary. It's a daily recording of events, or it could be a daily quote or a weekly fly fishing lesson. It's some form of written content, accompanied by pictures and video for enhancement.

A website may include a blog, as many do. A website has the addition of other services such as an online store, or HR profiles. However, some people have websites and blogs that are interchangeable. It's not important which is which, just that they are functioning the way they should.

Blogger is Google's blogging platform, which has been around and been free since the beginning of blogging, but Blogger is not as popular as it once was. It lacks some of the functionality of WordPress and the youth appeal of Tumblr. Blogger is simply the blogging platform for the previous generation. Now those users have either given up blogging or moved to WordPress where they can have a self-hosted website that functions as a professional business website.

Tumblr is the Millennial's answer to blogging. It's been around since 2007 and was bought by Yahoo. Tumblr is much more suited to images and short form content than the long form content favored by WordPress. It is much more aligned to some forms of content such as fashion, gaming, and pop-culture. These can be very popular and well represented on Tumblr.

Because the traffic isn't overwhelming and mainly consists of a smaller demographic, some niches with the right brand strategy can carve out a place for themselves on Tumblr. It's responsive, interactive, and easy to use. Plus it indexes well for search engines.

WordPress is the stiff old CEO of the blog world. Its more formal, clean, minimalistic designs have become the "fresh look" for current bloggers. WordPress has a lot of functionalities and is far more than a blog. It is a fully functioning website design, capable of doing anything a website does. You can pay for hosting through any number of sites that host your website for you.

Compared with Blogger and Tumblr, WordPress is much more difficult to change and manipulate. However, it is possible to make changes to your site yourself, just not as easily as on Blogger or Tumblr.

Another advantage of WordPress is their many responsive layouts. This is critical in today's world where so much of the time people are accessing your website from a mobile phone or tablet. But when thinking of WordPress, it's best to think of it as a website that includes a blog, rather than merely a blogging platform. Yes, your blog is incorporated into it, but merely as another piece of content in your overall offering.

Squarespace is yet another blogging platform which a latecomer to the scene. They have managed to pick up some high profile clients and are particularly known for their amazing graphics. However, many of their designs are not responsive, and that is not acceptable in today's mobile-driven world.

One thing you don't want to try to do is migrate your customer from one platform to another. If you start on Squarespace and realize they can't meet your needs for responsiveness, it will be very difficult to change to Wordpress or Tumblr.

Instagram

This is definitely the place to be now and into the future. This is where the millennial crowd is hanging out. And these young people don't mince words. In fact, it seems they barely use words at all. Everything for them is about images. That's what Instagram does so well. It's like Twitter and Pinterest combined at the speed of the new Millennium.

There are 180 million Instagram posts sent every day. How many of them is your business sending out? The answer should be zero, or twenty or more per day. If you're not prepared to engage, or if your business isn't right for Instagram, you should steer clear until you're ready. It's not a place you can just hang out and watch, you need to participate.

To participate, you need to have good visual content. Your images need to represent your brand and be consistent. People should be able to look at one of your pictures and say, "Oh that's a _____ photo."

Young people can be unforgiving and have short attention spans, and they own this space for now. In five years, they will no longer be so young and the new batch of youngsters will have moved on to something else, but for now the instant visual is King.

If your business has any visual element, be it a car dealership, real estate, or a cat rescue, you need to invest in some good photographs or graphics. Hire someone who knows how to take good looking pictures and keep them busy.

But the most important thing you can do to develop a presence on Instagram is to get your audience working for you. If you're a shoe manufacturer, reward people for taking a picture of them wearing your shoes and posting it on Instagram. Images of celebrities engaging with your product are even better. Forget the story, just get the picture.

Even if your product isn't particularly visual, find a way to obtain an image. For instance, an unknown young poet started posting pictures of his poetry, written out in text on Instagram. It became a huge sensation. Teen girls were flocking into bookstores looking for this guy's poetry, only to be told that the bookstore had never heard of the poet. You can bet they figured out who he was pretty quick.

Snapchat

This is another visual platform that is one of the go-to apps for Millennials. The difference between Snapchat and Instagram is that Snaps have a time limit. Some basic snaps will disappear in a matter of minutes. More complex Snap Stories have a 24-hour shelf life at most.

So how can your company benefit from a media that only lasts a day? There are some ways to take advantage of this platform, and the more creative, the better. First, you're going to have your content stored on another platform like Instagram to begin with.

There are several things you can do to leverage this system. For example, let's go back to the MinMax table. Maybe you start snapping photos or short videos and sending them out once a day 30 days in advance. They only stick around for a few minutes and then poof they're gone. If the customer missed it, they could go to Instagram or the Umea website.

Or maybe you create a serial campaign where you snap a piece of the content every hour for 8 hours until 8 pieces of advancing "story" have been shown. People who catch it on snap three will want to see what was on snap one or two. Now they need to go to one of your other sites.

You can also have people snap pictures and send them in during a time limit. These are the type of strategies that young people especially get excited about. They can't stand to miss out on something (well who can really?). Keeping them guessing about what might be going on is one way to ensure their engagement. And Snapchat is uniquely positioned to do that because they can't just look it up later. They have to be focused on you all the time.

Vine

Vine is a video-based platform owned by Twitter. The premise is that you take six seconds worth of video in 1-2-second increments and then the six seconds is compiled together and the video plays in a continuous loop over and over.

This can produce some great animation to what would otherwise be a static image. They are fast and not intended for high-quality video.

There are a lot of ways businesses are using Vines. For instance going back to MinMax. You could make a six-second video of the coffee-table opening to the desk. Then make one of its opening to the table and so on. This snippet is enough to whet people's appetite and make them want to explore more on your site.

Some brands are using Vines to show a series of products like books, shoes, pants, backpacks. It could be a trivia question and answer. Or it might be something just for fun. Not everything has to be about business. Something that's relevant, but fun can be a good way to engage your audience.

YouTube

YouTube has been around for years providing video of everything and anything. Having a YouTube channel is a must for any business. Very simply, YouTube takes the visual content that Vine, Instagram, Snapchat, and Pinterest do and makes it limitless. If it takes you two hours to demo your newest software program, fine, take two hours.

It takes the best parts of the visual content and collects them all in one place. Plus Google owns YouTube, which is always a bonus when it comes to SEO. It counts for more in searches with Google, and it shows up in a Google search. Besides YouTube is the second largest Search Engine, second only to its parent Google. It has an Alexa of 4 in the US and 3 globally.

Just like Google gives you the answer to any question, YouTube demonstrates how to do almost anything on video. And if you just need a laugh, there's everything from parody to cat videos.

Some other benefits of YouTube are the great analytics. It's also monetized. You can actually get money for video views. For some organizations, this is a major source of revenue.

Of course, you need to have some YouTube Videos on your YouTube Channel, but what kind are right for your company? Remember, we talked previously about the blender company CEO who regularly posts videos of different everyday items being blended in one of his machines? Here are some other ideas:

• Interviews- These can be interviews with anyone from the CEO to the front-line employees. In fact, they should be everyone. The more team members you have on video, the better. It makes people feel that you are human, not just a company.

• Overview of the company- What does your office look like? What's the atmosphere like? Do you have a warehouse? Do you have trucks coming and going? What does a day in your office look like? Make a video bring customers into your business even if they're on the other side of the world.

• Product Demonstration- How does your product work? Does it need to be assembled? If so how is that done?

• Webinar- Are you hosting a webinar? Make a recording.

• Advertising- Do you have television ads? They can be included on your YouTube channel. Creative ads do well on YouTube. For example, you'll find a great collection of Super Bowl ads here.

• Podcasts- Are you making series of podcasts? Those can be put on your channel.

These are just a few ways that YouTube can be used to bring people closer to your company. Ways that will help them become engaged with you and your mission.

Flickr

Flickr is another photo site. What makes it different from Instagram and Snapchat is the ability to organize photos into albums. The difference between Flickr and Pinterest is that on Flickr you are organizing your own photos, while on Pinterest you are curating other people's photos.

On Flickr, you can create groups of people who are interested in the same type of photos. For instance, let's say the National Zoo has a new baby panda (or twins). They can give users access to their Flickr photos of the cubs. Then users can share them on their own social media sites and spread the news. Or zoo patrons can create their own albums of the cubs.

Any business that has a visual, tangible product absolutely needs good quality pictures of each of their products. You can upload your photos to Flickr as a safe place to store all of them. This will allow your staff to access pictures when necessary.

If you have a service business, you can still post pictures of your staff. Take pictures at parties, and picnics. This lets people know that you are a real person, not a robot. Or maybe you could take pictures of your business. Your office, and the people that work there. Or, even employees working with your customers. All of these pictures can be loaded to Flickr so they can be saved. It's like giving your customers access to your picture albums.

SOCIAL MEDIA MEASUREMENT SYSTEMS

Hootsuite

Hootsuite is a social media dashboard that provides a way to oversee and administer a wide span of data across your online social media networks. A single login allows you to post to numerous sites at scheduled times. This makes it easy to contribute content to various sites. It also means a simple and easy way to observe and monitor all the content you are producing. You are able to keep an eye on trends across multiple platforms while also being able to observe what your competitors are posting. What's more, Hootsuite provides for scheduling of posts. In addition to being able to post on five sites at the same time, you can also set a timeline to post automatically in the hours you may be asleep or away from the computer.

To begin using Hootsuite you login to the program, then login to your other social media sites via Hootsuite. Currently, Hootsuite works with Facebook, Twitter, Google+, LinkedIn and Instagram. You can purchase an app to include other apps like YouTube. Once it has been set up all you need to do is monitor it on a daily basis. They have several comprehensive analytics programs that can provide you with results driven data that you can use to make any alterations.

Use your content calendar to determine what content needs to be created for each network, and when it needs to be set up. You can create your content, and pre-schedule it to go out at the agreed upon time. You can also save content to be used over multiple times so you don't have to re-create it unless it changes. In addition to the pre-determined content, you may want to look for things that come up unexpectedly. Testimonials from clients, Instagram pics of a customer using your product, a great quote that you want to share with your audience. You can add this additional content as well by using Hootsuite. If you have Hootsuite for Chrome installed on your Google Chrome Browser, you can use it to instantly add anything you find that you want to curate. You can schedule it for a specific time, or you can "auto-schedule" it and Hootsuite will pick the perfect time based on the social network you have chosen.

Hootsuite also comes with a large group of add-on applications that can allow you to monitor other networks, such as Flickr, WordPress, and Vimeo. They also have an additional analytical application that can be added to the program to give even more options for evaluation. You can also assign different people to your team to different tasks within the Hootsuite program.

Sprout Social

Sprout Social is a social media dashboard that has a lot in common with Hootsuite. It has a scheduler that allows the user to schedule posts across multiple platforms such as Twitter, Facebook, Google+, and Instagram. It also has an integrated widget on the Google Chrome Search Engine that allows it to schedule posts from anywhere on the web. One difference is that while Hootsuite provides its "auto schedule" for free on any plan, Sprout Social requires you to pay for a premium plan to get their auto scheduling module.

Sprout Social, on the other hand, has a system that monitors your incoming conversations and mentions. It collects them in a special column so you can always be aware of what people are saying about you on the web. Sprout Social comes integrated with Zendesk, UserVoice, and Salesforce, while these are add-ons for Hootsuite.

Sprout Social has a very well developed set of analytics available. Their programs are actually stronger than the Hootsuite analytics unless you pay extra to get the additional analytics. Sprout Social requires each individual to pay for a personal account at 59.00 per month. This could become very expensive depending on the size of your team. The next level of membership is 99.00 per person per month, and then 500.00 for a team of 3.

Sprout Social has a group of training programs, which is growing on a regular basis. You can learn skills like:

- Social Media Demo for Marketers

- The Social Business: Highlights from the Sprout Social Index

- Are You Maintaining a Healthy Twitter Feed?

- Twitter Action Plan: Top Tips

- The Social Customer Infographic

The Sprout Social Site is very clean and fresh with a lot of springy green accents and easy to read fonts. It's easy to see everything at a glance, but it doesn't look busy or cluttered. Clearly a lot of thought and planning went into the design of the site.

TweetDeck

TweetDeck is a social media management resource which works exclusively with Twitter. One of the main advantages of TweetDeck is that it is responsive for both desktop and mobile. You can even have multiple sessions of TweetDeck running at the same time, one on a tablet, and one on your desktop. Or you can use TweetDeck on your phone while you're at lunch and away from your desk.

Although TweetDeck only manages the Twitter application, without it you would be hard pressed to get anything useful out of Twitter. You can set up multiple feeds in TweetDeck to run simultaneously. One column that is automatically created is the "Scheduled" column that shows Tweets you have scheduled through TweetDeck, Hootsuite, or whatever.

Another column you can set up is the "Mentions Feed." Anytime your @yourname comes up, it will feed into a separate column labeled "Mentions." You can also create a special column for Hashtags. For example if you had the hashtag #MinMax set up, you could set up a column just to look for mentions of that hashtag. Or you can set up a column for a person on your team, or for your boss by searching by their @mybossJr. Then create a separate column just for that person so you can see any time they are mentioned.

You can also create a feed column for each one of your Lists from Twitter. In Twitter, you can set up lists to identify different people, either demographically, or by product type. Use whatever way you want to break them down so that instead of trying to manage tens of thousands of people in one big mass stream, you have smaller lists. For example, Umea Furniture might have each of its followers set up on a list based on the types of furniture they have bought in the past.

- MinMax

- Cabinets

- Case Goods

- Soft Goods

- Decorative

- Children's

- Other

Each person gets put into one of the lists so they can be analyzed and reviewed more easily.

Another task you can perform in TweetDeck is scheduling tweets. You can set up a tweet, add an image, and schedule it for the future. You can also retweet and add your own quote before you tweet, right from the TweetDeck Dashboard. Also, you can favorite tweets or reply to tweets from within the TweetDeck app. Essentially, you use this app instead of going to the main Twitter feed, which may show hundreds of tweets coming in every minute.

Agorapulse

Agorapulse is a social media dashboard that while perhaps not as well known as Hootsuite or Sprout Social, nonetheless remains a viable option for a business looking to manage its presence online. Agorapulse favors clean lines and straightforward design. This serves to enhance the ease of use of the Agorapulse dashboard and reduces the learning curve.

Agorapulse currently works with feeds from Twitter, Facebook, and Instagram. It allows users to track shares and mentions on the three networks. If they identify a user who has commented in the past, they can access that person's profile and get a history of his/her previous comments. This helps to address customer with a personal knowledge of their history with the company. You are also able to reply or forward comments directly from the dashboard, so responses are made promptly. If the commenter is complaining about something, especially an issue they have experienced in the past, seeking to resolve the issue with a view to that context is supremely important.

This timely and thoughtful response will also track well to any other customer who is looking at your company feeds. Always keep in mind that in the digital age, customers are able to see things like customers who complain on Twitter feeds.This can make them feel uncertain about doing business with a company who has received a lot of seemingly valid complaints. However, if your company responds with alacrity and offers a solution, potential customers can feel good that your company will take care of them as well.

In addition to monitoring incoming communications, Agorapulse also has a publishing page that allows you to set up your content and publish it to Facebook, Twitter, and Instagram. It has an embedded content calendar, so you can see all of your campaigns laid out by date and time prescheduled on a monthly basis.

Their reporting tools allow you to analyze your performance on the three networks, and to do A/B split testing for results regarding your content. The reports are easy to read in PowerPoint format. They also have the ability to compare your results to your competitors to see how you stack up.

Agorapulse also has a CRM tool that allows you to identify your best customers and biggest contributors. You can see at a glance who's supporting you with retweets, favorites, likes, and social sharing.

Finally, this program allows you to incorporate Facebook contest apps to make up a contest for customers to take quizzes, enter a photo contest, take a personality test, and get a coupon and more. While this feature only works with Facebook at this time, it is a very promising way to engage with customers.

Simply Measured

Simply Measured provides analysis and management for the largest number of different social networks of any provider. They have tools that work with Facebook, Twitter, Google+, Instagram, YouTube, Vine, LinkedIn, and Tumbler. They have reports that monitor performance in a comparative manner across all networks. They also have individual reports for each of the platforms, and reports for your paid marketing efforts. This is a network designed for large companies with hundreds or thousands of employees, and millions or even billions in revenue.

Simply Measured is the only social marketing analyzer that has reports specially designed for the following vertical markets:

- Retail

- Financial and Insurance

- CPG

- Sports

- Restaurant

- Media and Publishing

- Travel and Hospitality

- High Tech

- Telecommunications

These reports provide insight like no other because they are prepared for a particular market. They are able to compare your performance against your competitors. Determine the success of your efforts across multiple social networks and profiles. Find out what content makes your campaign work best. Remain focused on the influencers and trends most important to your brand. Measure the effect of your ad spend on your overall strategy. Keep tabs on your local presence. Listen to sentiment and customer service concerns about your brand.

The company has a large compliment of resources that they make available to their clients. They provide e-books for Twitter, Facebook, and Instagram analytics. They develop annual reports on social media trends and strategies. Simply Measured also provides explanations regarding the most popular networks. Strategy kits are available for Facebook, Twitter, Instagram, and general social media. They have three professionally developed White Papers. They have twenty-seven different social media guides covering a wide range of topics.

All of the many benefits of Simply Measured come at a high cost. This program is targeted at large companies that can afford an $800 per month fee.

SEARCH ENGINE OPTIMIZATION

How to select keywords for your campaign

You're ready to create the content for your campaign, and you know you need to include keywords so that the search engine will be able to find your information. You also plan to advertise, and you need to plan keywords for that purpose. Here are the steps you need to take to select your keywords:

1. Think like your customer.

Here is where you are going to pull out those customer profiles we created. We already have Penny Young-Professional and Tim Tiny house. You will need to create at least a tertiary profile.

Think like Penny and Tim, when they get ready to look for furniture for their small places, what keywords are they going to search for? Make a list of as many possibilities as you can. Here are a few to get you started:

- Coffee Table

- Bench

- Dining Table

- Desk

- Small Table

- Portable Table

- Multifunction Furniture

2. You should be able to come up with a lot more than that. You need to have 5-20 keywords for your advertisement. Try to think of 13 more keywords.

3. Now you need to decide how general or specific you want this search to be. In this case, general would be the way to go. Umea is a large furniture store with thousands of different products. If Penny and Tim happen to land on some other page from Umea, instead of the MinMax page, it won't hurt Umea.

4. Group similar words into themes. So far, we have three themes here:

- General Furniture

  - coffee table

  - bench

  - dining table

  - desk

- Small Furniture

  - Small Table

  - Portable Table

- Multifunctional Table

5. Plan for negative keywords before you start to set up your advertisement. Let's say, Umea sells all kinds of furniture, but they do not sell mattresses. If someone searches for furniture you want to be found, but if they search for mattresses you don't want to waste your ad dollars on something you don't sell. By making "Mattress" a negative

keyword, anyone who uses the word mattress in their search will NOT be directed to your site.

6. Which keywords does your competition use?

There are several websites that can help you analyze your competition so you know you have a competitive list of keywords. Sites like www.spyfu.com, and www.SEMRush.com, www.compete.com, and www.rankingcoach.com. All of these sites allow you to analyze your competition for many things including their advertising and keyword usage.

7. Have you covered all the possibilities including adjacent products and industries that might make legitimate searches?

The best way to do that is to do technology mapping, followed by text clustering.

> • Technology mapping is thinking about the different technologies that are "neighbors" of the product/service you have, and continuing to move further away on the map. So let's think about Penny and Tim again. Penny lives in a small apartment in the city, and Tim lives in a tiny house that can be anywhere. They aren't in the same neighborhood, but they are definitely on the same map.

> • Tim's next-door neighbor is an RV, and just beside that is a yurt.

> • Penny's next door neighbor is a larger apartment, and next to that is a townhouse.

> • Right between Penny and Tim is a mother-in-law suite. A little closer to Penny is a small free-standing office in someone's backyard. A little closer to Tim is a small free-standing art studio in someone's back yard.

• So now we've identified several adjacent products that might be good targets for our MinMax furniture. RVs, Yurts, other apartments, townhouses, mother-in-law suites, small home offices, and home art studios.

• Text clustering is using the same ideas to align your text with these new markets. Do you need to add, RV furniture, or yurt tables to your keyword search list?

By now you should have a solid list of keywords that you feel will do well in a search for your product. Now you have to write your copy and your content. This is where you want to proceed with caution when it comes to using those keywords. Search Engines no longer allow you to "stuff" your content full of keywords. In fact, they actively punish people who do so.

They want their customers to be able to do a search using any combination of words they can think up, and come up with the perfect thing. They are always changing their algorithms to prevent people from producing terrible copy, content, and websites, just to try to satisfy the search parameters.

To keep the search engines happy, what you need to do is think like your customer, and write your copy and content based on what Penny and Tim need. If you understand the keywords that you need, and how they apply to your product and solve Penny and Tim's problem, there's no reason you should not be able to write beautiful content that incorporates the keywords organically.

You also need to keep in mind that some of the new changes to the Google algorithm favor long content over short. Your content, be it a blog or any content on your site, needs to be at least 2000 words long. Google does not appreciate shabby 300-word posts anymore. Short content doesn't provide the information searchers are looking for. It is neither informative nor strong, so it doesn't line up with Google's current requirements. That may change in the future. Customers may complain about posts that are too long. All Google wants is for their searchers to be happy and satisfied with their search.

To satisfy the current requirements, make sure your content is on point with your topic. The best content is engaging and informative from start to finish. Two thousand words of nonsense will not do. Neither will boring, lifeless posts using passive voice. Using the Umea example, you're a furniture store, you don't need to write about ice cream or polar bears. Stick to furniture and things directly related to furniture.

Using microsites to feed leads

Microsites are an excellent way to focus your campaign. They are especially effective for short-term projects, or for a special product offering. In our example, you decide to create a microsite to feature the MinMax brand of convertible, multipurpose furniture. The microsite consists of a page on your website that describes the MinMax furniture line, and then pictures of each piece of furniture in a stylized setting. There are links to the shopping cart. Once items have been placed in the cart and the customer is ready to checkout, they will be directed back to the Umea shopping cart page.

There are several reasons for creating this separate microsite within the overall Umea website.

- The MinMax brand has a distinct feel that is in keeping with the other Umea lines, but they want it to be seen as a complete stand-alone product offering. They have made some slight alterations to the color of the text and the navigation buttons to set the line slightly apart.

- The biggest advantage of the microsite is how it performs in your search engine optimization. You will be rewarded for taking the customer directly to the MinMax site when they put in the relevant keywords.

- You should always attempt to maintain a balance of having 50% of your searches land on the home or main page, and 50% land on pages embedded within your site. Having a microsite allows you to do this.

- It also allows you to use some of the infrastructure that already exists on your site, such as the payment page.

- Also, if they do decide they want to look at Umea's additional furniture line, they are already on the site and able to do so.

- In some microsite situations, you may have a landing page that is not attached to your regular website. This can work when you want to differentiate the information from your regular brand.

- You can also use a microsite for a short term offering, make people aware that once the time is up, the site goes away or becomes inactive. This is great for holiday microsites, like "Elf Yourself" from Office Max/Office Depot. Once the holidays are over, you can't submit any more pictures, but when the holiday season start again, the elves will return.

White Hat and Black Hat SEO

It's important to understand the difference between White Hat and Black Hat SEO. Organizations that want to develop relationships with their customers, and increase engagement need to focus on White Hat SEO. White Hat SEO focuses on what the customer needs. It strives to bring people to your site and have them stay, not just land there and then bounce. It provides content that immerses visitors in a shared vision. Best of all, the search engines love it.

Black Hat by contrast involves using means which are nefarious and underhanded and violate the search engine's policies to attempt to gain a favorable search engine rank. They have no interest in enthralling searchers or customers, they just want clicks and high rankings.

The main problem search engines have with black hatters is that they ignore the needs of the searcher, and only focus on attempting to get their product to the top of the list. This frustrates customers who expect to be able to get a good answer when they use the Search Engine. If they don't get the answer they want they will use another search engine. Google can't have that. They will do what they have to do to punish people who use Black Hat tactics. They change their algorithms to penalize people who take advantage of the system.

This doesn't make the White Hatters too happy either. They can be caught in the cross-fire and receive an undeserved penalty from the search engine. Also, they have to keep changing their content to adjust to the new rules created to thwart the Black Hatters.

When it comes to using White Hat SEO methods, there are no easy shortcuts. It means optimizing your content in a way that is genuine, and puts the needs of the searcher above any possible short-term gains. This means contributing quality content and being upfront when seeking to establish your brand online. While this is more painstaking, and may deliver less progress in the short term, the payoff is happy customers and search engines. White Hat SEO is the best avenue to pursue when it comes to Search Engine Optimization.

Some Examples of White Hat Strategies:

Produce long, in-depth content that seeks to fully and accurately answer searchers questions.

- Keep your content fresh. Even evergreen content needs to be refreshed periodically to make sure it's up-to-date

- Make sure your link profile is stellar. An excellent link profile has well-curated backlinks from high authority sites and no spammy backlinks. Backlinks that take people to unhelpful sites will make you look bad to the reader and to Google. Links that have been disabled, and links to spam are obviously not a good thing.

- Make sure you have high-quality anchor text. The text that is high-lighted in blue and shows people where to link is your anchor text. It needs to be diverse, not saying the same thing over and over. It needs to be branded with your site's page name, so people will know where they're going and when they have gotten there. It also should be diluted with other surrounding words so it doesn't appear like "keyword stuffing."

- The anchor text can carry your brand from an authority site.

- The anchor text can be combined with other keywords to make a stronger anchor.

- Semantically relevant anchors use words that are similar to the keywords but not exact.

Black Hat SEO Tactics

- Spamdexing, repeating unrelated phrases to manipulate the index.

• Adding irrelevant keywords to the content just to get extra hits.

• Repeating keywords in an inorganic way that reads like gibberish, and provides no value.

• Hide text, hide links, or use tiny text to hide the junk you've put on the site.

• Cloak your content from the search engine so it's not the same as what the customer sees.

• Bait and Switch after a site has reached a high rank. This is where you use White Hat tactics until your site ranks high, and then cram a lot of junk on when it has a high rank.

• Duplicate content of or mirror a site. Everyone hates this, it just make you look disorganized or desperate. Focus on getting users to your quality content.

• Spam Blogs are blogs that may appear to have genuine content, but when you read them, it's nothing but one long advertisement. The same thing is repeated day after day with a new blog title to try to entice new, unsuspecting readers.

• Trackback spam is where people exploit the trackback system to send out spam. The trackback system is great. It lets you know when people have linked to a piece of your content. It allows you to thank the person or find out how they used your link. It also allows you to monitor anyone who might be misquoting you or linking to you inappropriately. However, when Black Hatters use it to get you to come to their spam site, it is annoying and time consuming. It causes some bloggers to have to turn off their trackback feature, and miss out on legitimate trackbacks.

• Pingback spam is the same thing as trackback spam, only it is internal to WordPress only.

• Referrer spam is where you make a lot of web site requests using a fake referrer URL. This inadvertently leads to links back to the spammer's site. The search engine finds these links and assumes they are legit and gives credit to the spammer for having a good link.

• Link farms are pages that attempt to "harvest" links from high-profile sites, and have no purpose other than farming those links.

• Cybersquatting people who buy up high-profile domain names so they can sell them back to companies who need them.

While it may seem like Black Hat webmasters benefit in some way from their underhanded dealings, the truth is all they do is make users angry. They ruin their own reputation and make it harder for everyone to do legitimate business.

SEARCH ENGINE MARKETING

Landing Pages for SEM

A landing page is a crucial aspect of your business's SEM in the online world. When operating well, a good landing page can represent a first point of contact with your business and its operations. So, what makes a good landing page? Good content.

Some characteristics of a good landing page:

- A clear message that intrigues and informs your customer.

- An attractive presentation that matches your brand image.

- Clear content that invites visitors to engage, participate, and share.

- Crisp, clean content regardless of the complexity of the information provided.

- The page must have a modern look and feel.

— No outdated or blurry gifs or graphics.

— Navigation that is functional and dynamic.

— Links and contact details are in service, up-to-date, and current.

- Complimentary design that doesn't clash with your overall web design.

- A color scheme that compliments the logo and other marketing materials.

An attractive landing page is one the most important features your business can have. Devoting time to its maintenance is an important management task that requires dedication and creativity. Ensuring it is built right the first time will make this ongoing task of maintenance all the easier as time goes on.

Cost per Click and Bidding

Cost per Click (CPC) is another important avenue to consider when beginning to build or enhance your online operations. It should be scalable so it will grow with you, and it should provide a useful measurement tool over time. The success of the campaign is demonstrated by increased traffic to the site. The most important thing to understand about CPC marketing is bidding.

CPC allows you to pay for ads in a more cost-effective way, and learn exactly where and when your business connected with a consumer. This is because unlike other forms of advertising, using CPC bidding means you only pay after your ad has been clicked. The key is, you have to set a Price per Click before the advertisement runs and then pay each time someone clicks on your ad.

The bidding process involves trying to pay the lowest Price per Click possible to achieve the highest rank on the search engine. One way internet marketers can do this successfully is by making sure they are getting the highest scores possible from Google. The search engine doesn't look just at the price the bidder is willing to pay. They also evaluate the website to determine its worth. Is it full of strong long-form content which is informative and matches the keywords associated with it? If so, it will get a higher score. Does it have a strong base of links from high-authority sites? This will also improve the score. Finally, is the description complete with helpful information such as address, phone number, and hours of operation? These things mean a site can score higher than a competitor who is willing to pay more.

Having all of your website ducks in a row can mean that your company winds up paying much less for cost per click marketing than your competitor. On the other hand, lazy or sloppy websites mean you will have to pay more for no additional benefit.

Using Google Analytics

When it comes to SEM analysis, few tools are more useful than Google Analytics [GA]. It allows you to measure your relative growth in the market. The 'entry level' use of the service is free, but paid upgrades exist. It is a useful starting point if you want to build your social media toolkit. It has analytical elements that will help you make informed decisions. The great thing about GA is the scale of the operation. While other tools for analytics exist, using the Google-backed tool means you enjoy the assets that exist within the company.

Starting out, you may find the GA interface confusing. The display is similar in appearance to a dashboard. There are so many options, you may feel overwhelmed. However, over time you'll find certain features and elements of GA can be "sectioned off." This is an important consideration as you decide how many individual websites you wish to list on GA. The site currently allows for 50.

A blog post or piece of information you have posted in a separate link can be visited by people via multiple avenues. GA lets you have a way to determine where the *organic* visits to your particular post or link are coming from. What this means is you'll be in a position to evaluate where and in what way your content is generating interest and attracting attention.

This is done in via a "page tag." A page tag is a piece of code embedded into your website which then keeps track of the clicks to and within your website. The only limitations are the users themselves. If a user has installed a plugin that blocks GA from receiving data about their visit to the website, your data will be skewed. If you're in a field where it is highly likely, your visitors will have the plugin installed, this might be a legitimate concern. However, such a concern can be regarded as minimal under normal circumstances.

You also need to decide if you will be using Google AdWords. AdWords is a service where Google and their partner websites promote ads across other websites. Ads featured underneath the AdWords umbrella use the combined websites to grow traffic and online awareness.

If you own or operate a small business, you should consider going beyond AdWords and use AdWords Express [AE]. Previously known as Google Boost, AE is a downscaled and more elemental version of AdWords. It means time and energy can be saved should you not have a need to deploy AdWords. This is an especially pertinent decision to make should you only have one website as opposed to the 50 AdWords allows.

IN-HOUSE OR OUTSOURCE?

Business marketers with broad experience in platforms

Experienced brand and campaign managers can often be the difference between a business's successful growth each quarter or stagnation. Therefore, it's vital to have the right person or team in place to manage this component. An important factor to consider is the experience the individual or team has managing the many platforms available for digital marketing today. Do you have a team with multiple people who are each expert at a specific platform, or do you have an individual who is forced to wear all of the hats?

Is either of these approaches really the best? Having a large group of highly specialized practitioners can leave a gap if someone becomes ill or leaves the company. In the other instance, having one person handle so many aspects that yield success can lead to ineffectiveness.

Currently, many of the top digital marketing experts are available at social media agencies. These may be a good option to help manage a variety of campaigns.

Experts at projecting brand value

What is the value inherent in your brand? Do you have the best prices in town? Do you have the highest quality? Do you strive for innovation that no competitor can match? There are many things that go into making up the value of your brand. These are company assets that need to be protected and projected.

It's up to the marketing person either in-house or outsourced to understand those unique qualities that give your brand value and to project them to your customers and competitors.

This can be done in many ways in the digital sphere. The successful brand manager is one that combines outstanding content with a robust social media strategy and uses them both to earn a high rank in SEO so that dollars spent on SEM get the most value possible. You should strive to have that person on the team … whether it's internally or externally.

They have experience managing campaigns

When it comes to managing a broad and wide campaign, having the experience and knowledge to do so confidently is all-important. It is not just a question or what to post, but at what time, where – and *why?* As previously mentioned, social media can be a game-changer when it comes to helping build a business's profile and boost profit; but it also can be a pitfall. A poorly worded message, an ill-considered campaign or even an inadvertently insensitive Facebook post could end up doing substantial damage to your reputation. A good Social Media Manager will be aware of these things and make sure those missteps don't occur

A Social Media Manager will coordinate social media output. He or she will also develop a content calendar and establish the long-term goals you have for your business. He or she manages the marketing staff which may include SEO/SEM experts, digital marketing analysts, ghost writers, a photographer and graphic designer. They will showcase the product or service your business provides. They will ensure photos are taken so they look good on Instagram. Tweets will be direct and concise. Facebook and Google+ posts will be engaging. Content will be exciting. LinkedIn will paint the company as someplace everyone wants to work at.

A good Social Media Manager will obtain knowledge about newly emerging and growing trends within social media and the wider online sphere. They'll be in a position to advise you of it; and how best to pursue opportunities using it. This role may be as critical to your operational effectiveness as any of the other members of your leadership team. Skilled Social Media Managers are propelling their organizations out of obscurity and into the highest profile positions in their industries.

When it comes to the specific advantages a Social Media Manager can offer your business, few are more pronounced that the analysis and data they can provide. This is especially true when it's used to coordinate your efforts across multiple platforms. In the day-to-day of online management and content production, you may find yourself gaining new followers. You may also get a steady stream of comments and shares from users. But so what? How does that convert into revenue? A Social Media Manager can provide your organization with the insight to utilize and exploit these engagements. Businesses that understand their users and are able to use analysis to captivate their audience have a distinct advantage.

When you're small, outsource to save. When you're big, outsource for experts

Once you've achieved the steady growth you need, it's time to evaluate how you can sustain that momentum. Certainly, social media is something no relevant business can do without. However, it can occupy considerable time. This is where you must consider how well you can maintain your other duties and workload and continue to administer, monitor, and help grow your online brand.

Small- to mid-size companies can outsource some of their social media marketing, their SEO/SEM management, and their content marketing. You might think that you can't afford to hire someone to do this for you. Or, that you can do what needs to be done yourself.

However, you need to consider the opportunity costs associated with spending your time like this. What work are you failing to do, because you're spending your time doing something you're not an expert at? How much is your time worth? Every hour you spend trying to learn something someone else can do with ease, is an hour wasted. Social media agencies typically get things done more quickly and get better results. That's why they're in business. In the long run, small companies that outsource see more results from digital marketing.

No matter how hard you try, it will be difficult for you to be as effective at SEO/SEM as an expert. It's also difficult to create content written as well as that written by a professional writer. Developing the social and digital strategy can be complex as well. Determine where you need help based upon the strengths and resources already available to you.

Large companies can also benefit from outsourcing. Maybe you have a Social Media Manager that is running outstanding campaigns for you. But you may need fresh content, or want to exploit a new platform. A good social media agency will manage this as part of your content marketing engagement. You will benefit from having access to professionals who have the experience needed.

For example, let's say Umea wants to include an e-book on their website called "Finding Space in Your Tiny Place." It's about finding ways to utilize your space effectively (like buying multipurpose furniture from the MinMax line!) You could have your Social Media Manager write the book, but it would be much more cost effective to have your social media agency hire a freelancer to "ghost write" the book. They will make sure that in addition to being written well, it's also peppered with SEO content that will increase click throughs on your microsites.

They typically have a roster of talented ghost writers available to provide content. That way, none of your internal resources are expended. And let's face it, writing great long-form content like an e-book is not necessarily a cake walk. There is a specialized set of skills that are involved. Hiring an expert with the ability to write an excellent book will undoubtedly save money in the long run.

Conclusion

Being seen, being heard, and being memorable is a challenge every business faces. The sheer volume of traffic consumers are faced with creates the difficulty. People are constantly bombarded with information. Customers looking to make a purchase or engage a service have more options than ever before. But companies that know how to utilize content marketing, to make the most of their SEO/SEM positions, and exploit their social media platforms can stand out and achieve success.

The key to content marketing is to provide resources that enlist your customers' help in achieving your goals. They are so relevant and worthwhile that they generate buzz and establish your company as a market leader. They are so well produced that they solidify your reputation for quality. And they are so timely that they receive the visibility vital to success in the cluttered atmosphere of online marketing.

Let's face it, what we all want is what's best for us. Your customers and potential customers are no different. The place where the goals of *your* organization and the goals of your clients meet is the optimized location where engagement leads to visibility, understanding, and memorability. Great content is the key to that position.

Outstanding material provides solutions for everyday needs. The "why didn't I think of that?" answers that everyone is searching for. Or perhaps it's the answer to a question so obscure you thought no one would have a response. Either way, it's the right piece of information at the right time. It makes you want to know more. And it lets you know that you're not alone; other people are thinking, and talking, and sharing about what you care about. These are the feelings and experiences that create invested customers.

It all starts with having robust and comprehensive profiles for all of your target customers. Each of these profiles should be as real to you and your organization as any flesh-and-blood human being. You should know what they look like. How do they feel about themselves, the world, and their place in the world? Who they are demographically? What do they like? This and a host of other vital statistics are paramount.

Once you understand your ideal customer, as well as your secondary, tertiary, and quaternary customer base, you can create content designed to appeal to them. You can anticipate their needs and questions because they are "people" like anyone else. You can tailor your offerings to meet those needs and answer those issues.

But, you can have all the great content in the world—you can have world-class white papers, amazing infographics, or a Pulitzer Prize worthy e-book—but if no one knows it exists, it's just a waste of time. How do you broadcast this great message in a way that will lure in your customers? That's where social media comes in.

Social media is the voice of your campaign. It's the vehicle that lets people know you have something amazing to share. A way to connect with your target audience that entices them to learn more about the great thing you have to offer that is going to solve their problem.

In today's world, there is a social media application for every situation. It could be a global player like Facebook or Twitter with literally billions of followers, or it could be a niche player like Dribbble that caters to designers. Knowing where your target audience hangs out, and what they are seeing, listening to, and remembering, is essential to building the relationships that your business requires to be successful.

Fortunately, there is a host of tools that can be used to analyze the effectiveness of these different channels. They can also automate some of the processes to make sure you are interacting with your target customers at the time and place where they are most likely to be receptive to your message. Each social media channel has a different prime time when your efforts are most likely to pay off. Understanding your customer profile allows you to direct your efforts at the time where your ideal customer is most likely to be engaged.

When it comes to a whole campaign, you should use a content calendar to strategize about what social media channels you will use and at what times. This will give you an overview of your plan and allow you to make adjustments when, and if, they become necessary. It also allows everyone involved to see what the plan is, and enables them to coordinate their efforts within the scope of the overall strategy.

It's not enough just to utilize social media, even if you have great content to back it up. It's also vital to understand the nature of each channel and maximize the functionality to benefit your overall campaign. Knowing your audience will help you zero in on the right offerings to tantalize and convert. What is relevant on Twitter is not necessarily important on Google+. Each audience has its own agenda.

And of course when it comes to social media, being social is key! It's not a one-way street where you just dump information without ever interacting. To really succeed with social media, you have to dialog with your customers. Ask them a question, create surveys, formulate quizzes, and solicit feedback. Educate and entertain them. This is how you utilize your communication to create a memorable experience for your client.

Make sure every interaction is an opportunity, even if they have something negative to say. There is no bigger opportunity than an unhappy customer. Paying attention to adverse comments on social media is a great way to demonstrate your commitment to customer engagement. Assuring a dissatisfied customer that you hear them, and can solve their problem. Letting them know that you are going to make things right. These are fantastic ways to get their attention, and the attention of the millions of other people who are watching. Following up and resolving the situation is even more impactful.

The final piece of the puzzle is to ensure that your efforts at content marketing and social media engineering are recognized by the search engines. SEO is the key to making sure your online efforts are accessible to your potential customers. You can have the most amazing content in the world. You can have more followers, likes, and pins than anyone, but if the search engines don't recognize you, neither will your customers. To grab the attention of searchers you need to land in the top three, or at the most the top ten spots in a search. Effective SEO is the way to ensure that you are visible to your customers when they search for your product.

Hand-in-hand with effective SEO is search engine marketing. This is how you spend your marketing dollars to make sure you receive the highest rank possible. Optimized websites and advertisements allow you to get a higher ranking for less money. This is the best way to ensure you stand out from your competitors.

All three things; SEO/SEM, Content Marketing, and Social Media; have to harmonize to create an overall solution that will get you seen, heard, and make you memorable. If you use them correctly, your company can rise to the top of its field and dominate the marketplace.

Want More?

Hey, you made it! I appreciate that you took the time to finish this book. So, I'd like to give you a special gift.

I've worked with many businesses, executives, celebrities, and campaigns to help them define and execute strategies for social media, marketing and sales. Through this, I've been excited, motivated, fulfilled and humbled by their passion and drive.

If you want a free chapter of my upcoming book on how to sell more effectively using a simple and proven five step process, make sure to sign up for my email list to receive the advance copy.

Simply go to www.AmitAhluwalia.com or www.BrighterPixel.com, click on the Coffee, Tea, or Water button and send me your information. Make sure to let me know that you want the free advance copy of the chapter.

I would also love to hear about your success with your social media, SEO/SEM or content marketing campaign. Do the steps above and send me an email to let me know. I'm looking forward to hearing from you. Make sure you use the strategies you learned to engage your audience.

Be Seen, Be Heard, Be Memorable, because…Engagement Causes Action.

Amit

Founder of Brighter Pixel

BrighterPixel.com
Twitter @brighterpixel
Facebook Brighter Pixel
LinkedIn linkedin.com/company/brighter-pixel
AmitAhluwalia.com